Advanced MIDI User's Guide

Advanced MIDI User's Guide

Second edition

RA Penfold

PC Publishing

PC Publishing
4 Brook Street
Tonbridge
Kent TN9 2PJ
UK

Tel 01732 770893
Fax 01732 770268
e-mail pcp@cix.compulink.co.uk

First published 1991
Second edition 1995

© PC Publishing

ISBN 1 870775 39 2

British Library Cataloguing in Publication Data

A catalogue record for this book is available from the British Library

Printed and bound in Great Britain by Bell & Bain, Glasgow

Contents

1

Getting the message

As a crucial first step in exploiting MIDI, a reasonably comprehensive understanding of all the MIDI messages must be grasped. It has to be admitted that you are not likely to use all the MIDI messages, but you can not sort out the ones that are useful to you from the ones that are not unless you know what all the options are. A knowledge of MIDI modes is also essential. These determine how a MIDI device does (or does not) respond to any messages it receives. Both topics are covered in detail in this chapter.

Modes and channels

MIDI messages can be divided into two main categories: channel and system types. System messages are sent to every piece of equipment in the system and, where appropriate, each item of equipment will respond to a system message. Channel messages carry a channel number which is from 0 to 15 in terms of the actually binary number contained in the message. However, the convention has MIDI channels numbered from 1 to 16, and the MIDI channel number is therefore one higher than the actual channel value in the message. Unless you get into MIDI programming or hardware design, this slight anomaly is of purely academic importance. Unless stated otherwise, any references to channel numbers in this book are references to the conventional channel numbers from 1 to 16.

The MIDI modes govern how equipment responds to channel messages. System messages are treated in the same way regardless of which mode is selected. It is worth pointing out right from the start that MIDI is a framework within which all MIDI equipment must operate. It has to accommodate instruments, etc. ranging from some very simple types through to the most sophisticated units that modern technology can provide. This enables simple equipment to operate in the same system as more complicated units, but it also means that much of the equipment available has a less than full MIDI implementation. Modern instruments mostly have quite good MIDI implementations, but I have yet to encounter any MIDI unit that understands every MIDI message type. Early MIDI equipped instruments often have rather sparse MIDI implementations. Most instruments are not able to respond to all the MIDI messages, or even all the MIDI modes.

There is a slight complication with MIDI modes in that they have their original names, their new names, and mode numbers. All three are provided in this description of the MIDI modes, but thereafter they will only be described by their mode numbers.

Mode 1 – omni on/poly

This was formerly known as just "omni" mode, and it is the most basic of the MIDI modes. Virtually every piece of MIDI equipment supports this mode, and at one time it was the mode that instruments defaulted to at switch-on. Presumably because it is not a popular mode these days, many instruments now seem to default to a different mode at switch-on. Also, many instruments now have memory circuits so that they carry on from where they left off when they were last used. As these instruments do not start "from scratch" each time they are used, they do not really have what could realistically be termed a default mode.

The idea of mode 1 is to provide a means of ensuring that any MIDI device will be able to communicate with any other piece of MIDI equipment. This is achieved by having the channel numbers totally ignored. An instrument in mode 1 will respond to any messages on any channel. At least, it will respond to any messages that are within its repertoire of MIDI messages. The "omni on" part of the mode name indicates that this mode does not implement channelling. The "poly" part indicates that it is a polyphonic mode, and there is no limit to the number of notes that can be played simultaneously. Obviously in a practical setup there will be a limit to the number of notes that can be played at once. However, this is a limitation of the system hardware, and is not a limitation placed on the system by MIDI.

The manner in which the received notes are assigned to the voices of the instrument is something that varies from one instrument to another. In general, it seems to be the case that notes received via MIDI are assigned in the same way as notes played via the keyboard. This is largely academic anyway, since in this mode the instrument would normally be used with all its voices producing the same type of sound. There would seem to be no point in having more than one sound, since there is no way of ensuring that a given note will activate a particular voice of the instrument. This is a very basic mode which is largely devoid of versatility. It is little used these days. The sophistication of modern instruments is such that even when simply slaving one instrument from another, this mode might place constraints on what can be achieved.

Mode 2 - omni on/mono

This mode had no name under the old system of mode names, and it is a mode that many instruments do not implement. It is very much like mode 1, but as indicated by the "mono" part of its name, it only permits one note at a time to be played. With the system constrained to just one note at a time, this mode is the most basic of the four, and it is of little practical value. It is presumably included in the MIDI standard in order to accommodate monophonic synthesisers. As monophonic synthesisers were dying out just as MIDI was coming into being, few MIDI equipped instruments of this type were ever produced. There would seem to be little point in using a polyphonic instrument in this mode, as it would effectively be downgraded to a monophonic type.

With any MIDI instrument there is a risk that it will receive more notes than it can play, but this is obviously a major risk with a monophonic mode. MIDI does not set out any rules governing what should happen if an excess of notes should be received. This is up to the instrument designer. In days gone by it was often the highest note or the last one that was played. Many recent instruments seem to be designed to simply ignore any excess notes.

Mode 3 - omni off/poly

This is potentially the most powerful of the four standard MIDI modes. It was originally called "poly" mode. The "omni off" part of the name indicates that it implements MIDI channels. An instrument set to this mode will therefore respond only to system messages and channel messages that are on the correct channel. It will totally ignore any messages that are on the wrong channel. Some of the early MIDI instruments were restricted to operation only on channel 1, which was not very helpful. The idea of this mode is that it enables several instruments to be used, with each one on a separate channel. This permits independent control of up to sixteen instruments. Furthermore, this is a polyphonic mode, and each instrument can therefore play as many notes at once as its hardware permits. This is of little practical value if your instruments all have to operate on the same channel. Fortunately, all recent instruments seem to be able to operate on any desired MIDI channel, whether sending or receiving MIDI messages, giving the maximum potential from mode 3.

This mode is much used these days, and it enables you to do virtually anything you like. There is an obvious drawback in that you require sixteen polyphonic instruments in order to fully exploit it. However, even with three or four instruments this is still a very powerful mode. As we shall see later, many modern instruments effectively enable mode 3 to be fully exploited at relatively low cost.

Mode 4 – omni off/mono

This was originally called "mono" mode, and is still frequently referred to by its old name. It is basically just a monophonic version of mode 3, and as such might not seem to be particularly useful. In reality it is an extremely useful mode though, and for sequencing work it tends to be regarded as superior to mode 3 by many. The point to keep in mind here is that although this is a monophonic mode, it is only monophonic in the sense that it permits no more than one note at a time per channel. It permits an instrument to operate on the basis of having its voices assigned to different channels. These channels are normally consecutive, with the ability to select the base channel. With (say) an eight voice instrument set to have channel 4 as its base channel, it would occupy channels 4 to 11 inclusive.

Monophonic operation on each channel is a definite limitation, but the ability to have a different sound on each channel gives tremendous potential. In our eight voice instrument example, this one instrument can effectively operate as eight totally different monophonic instruments, giving eight note polyphonic operation overall. Two instruments of this type would be sufficient to occupy all sixteen MIDI channels, giving sixteen different sounds, and sixteen note polyphony overall.

Although this mode, by virtue of its one note per channel operation, is less potent than mode 3, it is more practical in that it enables a large number of sounds to be used in a system having just one or two instruments. This is a much more realistic prospect for most of us, than the mode 3 alternative of having a dozen or more instruments in the system!

It is important to realise that it is not necessary to have all the instruments in a system operating in the same mode. For the greatest versatility in a system having two or more instruments it is often best to have the instruments using a mixture of modes 3 and 4. As a simple example, for a piano piece plus a multi-part accompaniment, a polyphonic instrument set to mode 3 could provide the piano part, with one or two mode 4 instruments acting as the accompaniment. A couple of mode 4 instruments provides you with what is virtually a MIDI controlled orchestra.

When using mode 4 there are a couple of points worth bearing in mind. The first point to note is that far from all instruments support this mode. Modern instruments are much better in this respect than those that were produced a number of years ago. Some quite expensive and otherwise excellent instruments produced in the early days of MIDI lack mode 4.

The second point is that although an instrument can operate on several channels in mode 4, it might not give totally independent operation on each channel. Messages to switch notes on and off will certainly be on one channel only, and each one will only affect the appropriate voice of the instrument. Other message types sometimes affect all voices, regardless of what channel they are on. For example, with some instruments pitch wheel changes will affect all the instrument's voices regardless of which channel the messages are on. This is another area in which modern instruments are generally much better than those of a few years ago.

I suppose that strictly speaking an instrument which operates in this way is outside the MIDI specification, since it is operating in mode 4 on some messages, and mode 1 on others. Presumably the manufacturers, with some justification, feel that it is better to implement a feature in a slightly watered-down fashion than to simply leave it out altogether. It is still advisable to read the "small print" in MIDI implementation charts though, in order to ascertain exactly what can and can not be achieved in mode 4.

Multi mode

Although the MIDI standard only lays down the rules for four modes, many recent instruments implement a fifth mode. This is commonly called "multi" mode, but it is an unofficial mode, and consequently it does not have an official title under the MIDI specification. The name given to it is therefore subject to changes from one equipment manufacturer to another. The exact form it takes also varies slightly from one instrument to another, and some instruments actually have more than one version of multi mode available.

Although they might differ slightly in points of detail, there is one common denominator to all multi modes. They give what is effectively a polyphonic version of mode 4. In other words, each voice of the instrument can be assigned to a different MIDI channel, and will only play notes on that channel. Whereas mode 4 is restricted to one note at a time per channel, in multi mode it is possible to have several notes playing at once. The number of notes per channel is something that varies from one instrument to another, and some instruments have several multi modes that provide a range of options in this respect.

In the early days of MIDI the instruments were relatively simple, and something along the lines of a multi mode was presumably not included in the original specification as it was felt that the instruments of the day simply did not merit it. Today's instruments are much more sophisticated, offering something like thirty two note polyphonic operation in a few cases. Some form of multi mode is virtually essential in order to get the most from an instrument of this type. Even with something more basic like a six voice, six note polyphonic instrument, a multi mode can increase the versatility of the instrument. For example, instead of having single channel six note polyphonic operation, or six channel monophonic operation, it might sometimes be better to operate on the basis of something like three channel two note polyphonic operation.

Some multi mode instruments are more versatile than others. You might have one multi mode offering something along the lines of four note polyphony on four channels, or you might have several multi modes to choose from. Ideally a multi mode should have dynamic allocation of notes. As an example of how this works, suppose that an instrument is thirty two note polyphonic, and that it has eight voices. A basic set of multi modes might offer the option of four note polyphony on eight channels, eight note polyphony on four channels, or sixteen note polyphony on two channels.

With fully dynamic allocation of notes there would be just one multi mode offering thirty two note polyphony on eight channels. This is not quite as good as it sounds, since the thirty two note limit of the instrument would still apply, and would mean that there could never be more than thirty two notes sounding at anyone time. It would not there-fore be a true equivalent to eight thirty two note polyphonic instru-ments, which could provide up to two hundred and fifty six notes simul-taneously. On the other hand, how often would you really require more than thirty two notes sounding at once? Probably not very often.

The advantage of dynamic note allocation over having several multi modes is that it gives great flexibility without the need to keep switch-ing modes. If you require two notes on each of sixteen channels, and then twelve notes per channel on two channels the next instant, with dynamic note allocation there is no problem. In both cases our thirty two note limit has not been exceeded, and the instrument will automat-ically adjust itself to give the desired effect. With full dynamic note allo-cation, the instrument will always adjust itself to make the most of the available voices and channels, giving the required number of notes per channel provided the overall note limit is not exceeded.

In many cases there are slight limitations on any available multi modes. Perhaps with a thirty two note polyphonic instrument there would be a limit of sixteen notes per channel, not the full thirty two notes per channel. Even if there are some limitations of this type, or if an instrument has a multi mode that lacks any form of dynamic note allocation, it is still a great improvement over straightforward mode 3 or mode 4 operation. Some form of multi mode really is a great asset for any instrument that will be used for complex sequencing work.

On the face of it, multi mode is outside the MIDI specification, and should not be included on MIDI instruments. In truth these multi modes are within the MIDI specification, and are perfectly legitimate. When an instrument operates in a multi mode, it is effectively several instruments operating in mode 3. The fact that all the instruments are in the same box is of no real consequence. The system works the same whether the instruments are in sixteen different cases, or all in the same one. When used in a multi mode, each voice of the instru-ment acts as what is sometimes termed a "virtual instrument".

Getting the message

From this description of MIDI modes it should be apparent that MIDI has great potential. A computer or other MIDI controller can drive several instruments if desired, putting a sort of electronic orchestra at your disposal. A combination of MIDI and modern electronic musical instruments provides the sort of music making potential we could only dream about not so many years ago. MIDI is even more potent than you might think though, because it can handle a variety of message types, and it is not limited to simply turning notes on and off. There are a number of different MIDI message types, covering functions such as mode changes, timing signals, pitch wheel changes, and general control changes. Before looking at all these messages in detail it would be as well to consider the basic make-up of a MIDI message.

All MIDI messages start with an eight bit status byte (sometimes referred to as the "header" byte). The purpose of this byte is to indicate the message type, and in the case of a channel message it also carries the channel number. The header byte is divided into two four bit nibbles. For a channel message the most significant nibble (i.e. the fifth to eighth bits transmitted) carry the message identification code. By message code, I mean one that tells the receiving equipment that the message is a note on type, key pressure type, or whatever. The least significant nibble (the first to fourth bits sent) carries the channel number. As already pointed out, the binary value used here is actually one less than the conventional MIDI channel number. In other words, the binary number range is from 0 to 15, but conventional channel numbering is from 1 to 16.

Things are slightly different for system message header bytes. The most significant nibble is always 1111 in binary (240 in decimal), to indicate that it is a system message. The least significant nibble is not required in order to indicate a channel number, since these messages are sent on a particular channel. This leaves it free to indicate the type of system message (clock signal, system exclusive, etc.). Figure 1.1 shows how these two methods of message coding operate.

In many cases the status byte alone does not provide sufficient information, and it must then be followed by one or two data bytes in order to provide information about the note being played, how hard it is played, or whatever. In order to make it easy for equipment to differentiate between header and data bytes, header bytes always have the most significant bit set to 1, whereas it is always set to 0 on data

Channel message header byte

System message header byte

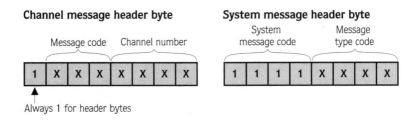

Figure 1.1 Header byte coding for channel and system messages

bytes. One practical consequence of this is that only three bits of the most significant nibble are available to designate the message type. This means that there is a limit of eight different message types; seven channel messages plus one code for system messages. It also means that there are only seven bits available to indicate the value in data bytes. In terms of decimal numbers this gives a range of 0 to 127. This is more than adequate for most purposes. However, as we shall see later it is possible to overcome this limitation.

The following sections list all seven channel messages. The figures in brackets after each message type heading are the binary and decimal values for the most significant nibble of the header byte. In the case of the binary figure, the four bits carrying the channel number must be added in order to give the full header byte. For the decimal value it is necessary to add one less than the channel number in order to obtain the total value for the header byte.

Note on (1001 - 144), note off (1000 - 128)

The most important MIDI messages are the note on and note off types. These are both three byte messages that have the status byte followed by two data bytes. In fact these two messages take the same basic form, and the different coding in the most significant nibble of the status byte is the only difference between them.

The first data byte carries the note number. Middle C is at a value of 60, and the system has semitone resolution. A data value range of 0 to 127 together with semitone resolution gives a coverage of over ten octaves, which should be ample. In fact few MIDI equipped instruments have such a wide compass, and in some cases (particularly with early sound samplers) the pitch range of the instrument is only a fraction of the full MIDI range. When scoring for acoustic instruments you need to keep in mind the limits of the instruments, and the situation is no different when dealing with electronic instruments. Some instruments simply ignore any out of range note messages they receive. Others transpose up or down one or more octaves so that they play the nearest suitable note within their compass. Although there might seem to be no point in having the note value in note off messages, this is absolutely essential. Remember that some MIDI modes offer polyphonic operation on each channel. A note off message must therefore make it entirely clear which particular note must be switched off.

Data byte number two carries the velocity value. This is a measure of how hard the keys of a keyboard instrument are played, with 0 representing minimum velocity and 127 being used when a key is played as hard as possible. Probably all current MIDI instruments have touch sensitive keyboards, or in the case of rack-mount expanders etc., are designed to respond to touch sensitivity information. This feature is absent on many older instruments though. Where it is not included, a dummy middle value of about 64 is used in all note on messages, and zero is used in note off messages. If an instrument does not implement touch sensitivity on notes received via MIDI, it will simply ignore the velocity byte, and play all notes at maximum volume. This data byte must always be included in note on and note off messages, as any equipment receiving these types of message will expect to receive them, and could malfunction if they were simply omitted.

The manner in which velocity bytes control the sound generator circuits of an instrument is up to the instrument designer. The velocity value normally controls the volume of notes, and it may well control other aspects of the sound generator circuit, such as the attack times of notes. The velocity value in note off messages could be used to control something like the decay times of notes, but in practice this data byte is usually of no practical significance. However, a few instruments which utilise this parameter are now produced. It is perhaps worth pointing out that although there are some 128 different velocity values, many instruments only seem to provide half a dozen or so different velocity levels. This is a vast improvement on having no touch sensitivity at all, but it does mean that the degree of control available is often noticeably less than the MIDI specification might suggest.

There is an unusual provision in the MIDI specification that permits notes to be switched off via note on messages having a velocity value of 0. Many MIDI users seem to be aware of this fact, but few seem to know its purpose. If you delve deep enough into the MIDI speci-fication it is possible to unearth the answer. On its own this provision is of little value, but it can be used in conjunction with another of MIDI's special provisions. It is permissible for one note on or note off status byte to be followed by several sets of data bytes. There would seem to be some advantage in doing this in that it enables more messages to be sent in a given period of time. In theory it would be possible to send a complete sequence using just one note on status byte followed by pairs of data bytes to switch notes on and off. In practice this is only possible if the sequence is restricted to operation on a single channel. Even so, this could help to avoid problems with MIDI "choke" (a subject which is considered in some detail in a later chapter). Apparently some

Note on message

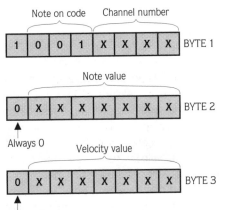

Figure 1.2(a) System of coding used for note on messages

sequencers do now use this method in order to streamline the data flow. Figure 1.2(a) and (b) show the way in which standard three byte note on and note off messages are organised.

Overall key pressure (1101 - 208)

This message consists of the header byte followed by a single data byte. The latter is a measure of how hard a key is pressed. Key pressure differs from velocity in that the velocity value is a measure of

Note off message

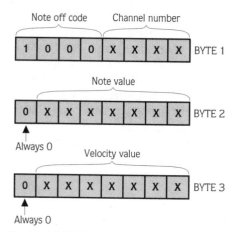

Note off code   Channel number

| 1 | 0 | 0 | 0 | X | X | X | X | BYTE 1 |

Note value

| 0 | X | X | X | X | X | X | X | BYTE 2 |

↑
Always 0   Velocity value

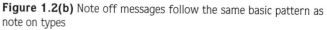

| 0 | X | X | X | X | X | X | X | BYTE 3 |

↑
Always 0

Figure 1.2(b) Note off messages follow the same basic pattern as note on types

how hard the key is pressed initially, and is actually a measurement of how fast the key moves. Key pressure is a measure of how hard the key is held down once it has hit its end-stops. In fact most keyboards will not send any key pressure messages until a key has been depressed for about half a second to a second. In normal instrument terminology, a keyboard that implements velocity values is a "touch sensitive" type, while one that implements key pressure has "aftertouch". The two are not mutually exclusive, and many modern MIDI keyboards have both of these features. Aftertouch is more common than it once was, but it is still falls some way short of being a standard feature. If a keyboard only has one form of touch sensitivity, then it invariably seems to be of the velocity sensing variety.

This form of key pressure sensitivity is a fairly crude type. It is a sort of average pressure value for all the notes playing on the channel in question. This gives only rather crude control over the dynamics of notes, but it is a definite improvement on having no control over the volume of notes after the attack phase. Of course, even on an instrument that implements aftertouch, with some sounds selected the aftertouch information might be ignored. This mainly happens with what might be termed percussive sounds, where there is no significant sustain period during which the aftertouch can control the volume. Harp and harpsichord sounds are a couple of good examples of these relatively short lived percussive sounds.

Polyphonic key pressure (1010 - 160)

Polyphonic key pressure differs from the overall type in that it provides separate key pressure values for each key, rather than simply using an average figure for all the notes playing on the channel in question. This requires the use of two data bytes after the header byte. The first of these data bytes is the note value, and this is the same value that was used in note on message that activated to note concerned. The second byte is the pressure value. This, like an overall key pressure value, varies from 0 for no pressure to 127 at maximum pressure.

Polyphonic key pressure is obviously a highly desirable feature. It is one that permits great expression to be put into one's playing, and stored for posterity in MIDI sequences. In the early days of MIDI even basic (velocity) touch sensitivity was by no means universal, and any form of aftertouch was extremely rare. The polyphonic variety was virtually unknown. Fortunately, some form of aftertouch is now becoming quite common, although the polyphonic type remains relatively rare. It is gaining in popularity though, and seems likely to become a standard feature in the not too distant future.

It is worth noting that aftertouch is not only implemented in keyboard instruments. It can be used with any MIDI instrument, including expanders and rack-mount units which have no built-in keyboard or other method of control. Obviously a unit of this type can not generate aftertouch messages, but it can be designed to respond to them. Several rack-mount instruments do recognise aftertouch messages, and even some low cost units respond to polyphonic aftertouch information. This is perhaps slightly ironic, with few (if any) low cost MIDI keyboard instruments having this feature.

Program change (1100 - 208)

In this context the word "program" usually refers to a set of sound generator parameters for a synthesiser. In other words, program change messages enable the sound of an instrument to be changed. We are talking here in terms of changing the sound from one preset sound to another preset sound, rather than a means of adjusting individual parameters of the sound generator circuit. Although the most common application of program change messages is to switch an instrument between sounds, they can be used in other ways. A typical example would be a MIDI controlled audio mixer, where program change messages can be used to switch from one set of "fader" settings to another. Program change messages are also much used with MIDI patch-bays and digital effects units.

A program change message consists of the header byte followed by one data byte. The data byte is the program number, and with a range of 0 to 127 this accommodates up to 128 different sets of sound generator parameters (or whatever). There is a slight problem here in that although the data value is from 0 to 127, the programs of the instrument might be numbered from 1 to 128, or even from something like A-1 to P-8. This can cause minor problems when trying to get one instrument to switch a second one to the desired program. However, the instruction manual for any instrument that uses program change messages should make the correlation between MIDI data values and the instrument's method of program numbering perfectly clear. Where there is no easy correlation between the two, the instruction manual often includes a simple conversion chart. Some careful planning and a few dummy runs can be needed in order to get everything right when using program change messages. Bear in mind that although MIDI can accommodate 128 different programs, some instruments do not support as many programs as this. Probably all modern instruments do, but many instruments from a few years ago only permit (typically) 64 or 100 different programs to be selected.

On the face of it, program changes are a useful feature, but one that is something less than spectacularly useful. It is a feature that should not be underestimated though. Suppose that a MIDI system has a six channel synthesiser operating in mode 4 or a multi mode, plus a second synthesiser operating in mode 3. This gives access to seven different sounds, which may be adequate, but during the course of a long piece you could well require more than seven sounds. Adding more instruments is one solution, but an expensive one. Also, the limit of sixteen MIDI channels means that this method can not provide more than sixteen sounds.

Using program changes and suitable instruments it is possible to use dozens of sounds in each piece of music. You simply switch from one sound to the next, as and when necessary, using a dozen or more sounds per channel if necessary. In our example system you are still limited to no more than seven different sounds at once, but for most types of music it is not necessary to have large numbers of sounds playing at once. If you wish to stretch your MIDI system to its limits, program changes are something you will almost certainly need to use a great deal.

Pitch bend (1110 - 224)

The MIDI note on/off commands give only semitone resolution, but the pitch of notes can be modulated via pitch bend messages. This is a three byte message, with the status byte carrying the appropriate message code and channel number. The next two bytes are the pitch change value. The two seven bit values in these data bytes are joined together to produce a 14 bit pitch change value. The first byte contains the seven least significant bits, while the second byte carries the seven most significant bits. Figure 1.3 shows how the three bytes of a pitch change message are interpreted by a device that recognises this type of message (which means virtually all MIDI equipped instruments).

Pitch bend message

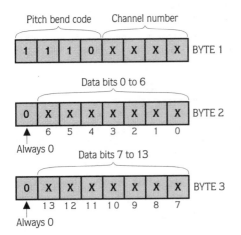

Figure 1.3 The system used in pitch bend messages

In terms of decimal numbers, a 14 bit binary number is equivalent to a range of 0 to 16383. This permits extremely fine control of the pitch. A pitch change of zero is obtained with the most significant data byte at a decimal value of 64 (01000000 in binary), and the least significant data byte at zero. In terms of the overall decimal number, this puts the zero modulation point at a value of 8192. As one would expect, values above 8192 increase the pitch, while values below 8192 reduce it.

It is doubtful if such fine control of the pitch is really worthwhile in practice. In order to make full use of the available resolution the pitch value would need to be varied by very small amounts. In fact it would ideally be incremented and decremented by one per pitch change message. This would require a vast number of messages in order to produce even quite modest changes in pitch. It is by no means certain that MIDI is capable of handling messages at such a high rate. In electronic terms MIDI is not particularly fast. Data is sent at a rate of 31250 baud (i.e. 31250 bits per second). With a start bit, a stop bit, and eight data bits, giving ten bits per byte, this represents an absolute maximum of 3125 messages per second. With many MIDI messages (including pitch change types) some three bytes long, this represents a maximum of slightly over 1000 messages per second. In order to increment the pitch change value from 0 to 16383 in steps of one would therefore take around sixteen seconds! Perhaps of more relevance, the pitch would be altered by such small amounts that the results of several successive pitch changes would be imperceivable, even to some having a very keen sense of pitch.

In order to give smooth pitch modulation with no perceivable stepping it is not necessary to have anything like 14 bit resolution. In fact the seven bit resolution of a single MIDI data byte is quite sufficient. It would seem that this has led to many instruments using only one data byte for pitch changes. Both data bytes must be sent as this is a requirement of the MIDI standard, but these instruments simply send a dummy byte having a value of 0 for the least significant data byte. When receiving pitch change messages these instruments simply ignore the least significant byte. Not all instruments operate in this way, and some do respond to all 14 bits of pitch change data.

There is a potential problem with pitch bend messages in that the original MIDI specification did not specify a precise relationship between pitch change values and the degree of pitch change that they should produce. This was left to the discretion of instrument manufacturers, and there are inevitably significant variations between instruments from different manufacturers. Normally a change of at least plus and minus one semitone can be achieved, and a range of as much as plus and minus three semitones is possible with some instruments.

There is now provision to set the pitch bend sensitivity via a MIDI control change message, and this should permit proper standardisation provided all your instruments support this feature. It may also be possible to alter the pitch bend sensitivity of your instruments via the front panel controls. With some instruments it is possible to enable and disable the pitch bend facility via a front panel control. This is useful, as it gives the option of having a slave instrument not follow pitch bend messages produced when operating the modulation wheel of the master instrument.

Control change (1011 - 176)

Most MIDI messages are specific in nature, but the control change messages are an exception. They can be used to alter any parameter that the equipment designer sees fit. This could be a parameter of the sound generator such as the attack time of an envelope shaper, or something more general such as the volume level. It is important to realise that there is no true standardisation of MIDI controls. A few conventions regarding their use emerged in the early years of MIDI, but even with these there were variations from one instrument to another, and they could not be taken for granted. Updates to the MIDI specification have made many of these conventions official, and have added many more recommendations. Unfortunately, the tidying-up of this aspect of the MIDI specification came too late to ensure that all instruments adhere to the recommended scheme of things.

What this means in practice is that a control change message that has the desired effect on one instrument might have a totally different effect on another instrument, or possibly even no effect at all. Some careful reading of instruction manuals is usually called for prior to making use of MIDI control messages. Using control change messages is likely to be more straightforward if all your instruments are of recent manufacture, as they should then utilise to the standard control assignments.

This type of message does not apply only to instruments, and can be used for items of equipment such as audio mixers, digital effects units, and patch-bays. The MIDI specification allows units such as these to utilise MIDI control change messages, even though the standard control assignments do not really apply to most of these units.

However, the MIDI implementation charts must make it clear if any non-standard control assignments are used. The implementation chart should also provide details of each control number's function.

The control change messages are three byte types which have the usual format of the header byte followed by two data bytes. In this case the two data bytes are first the identification number of MIDI control to be altered, and then the new value for that control. There is a slight complication to matters in that MIDI controls are, like the pitch change parameter, 14 bit types. This 14 bit resolution is achieved by using the controls in pairs, with one providing the seven most significant bits, and the other providing the seven least significant bits. In order to change all 14 bits it therefore takes two control change messages, and there is no way of changing all 14 bits simultaneously (there is a minimum gap of about one millisecond from one change to the next). Most changes require only one control change message though, since minor changes will often require only the least significant byte to be altered.

As already explained, 14 bit resolution gives extremely fine control, and it actually gives far finer control than most applications really require. Much control changing can therefore be done by altering the most significant byte and leaving the least significant one unaltered. With practical MIDI controls you often find that the hardware implements something well short of 14 bit resolution, and the least significant is often just ignored. Even the seven bits of the most significant byte might not be fully implemented, and I have encountered MIDI controls that have only five or six bit resolution. There is some debate in the MIDI world as to whether this pairing of controls should be continued, or whether they could more usefully be used as separate controls.

Where it is actually used, this pairing works on the basis of control numbers 0 to 31 being paired with control numbers 32 to 63 respectively. Thus control 0 operates in conjunction with control 32, control 1 is paired with control 33, and so on through to control 31 which is paired with control 63. The low control numbers carry the most significant byte - the high control numbers contain the least significant byte. Table 1.1 should help to clarify matters.

It will be apparent from this that half the MIDI controls (numbers 64 to 127) are not assigned to use as high resolution controls, or variable controls as they are often called. Control numbers from 64 to 95 (inclusive) are assigned to switch type controls. In other words, they provide a simple on/off function, and are used for such things as switching the low frequency modulation or the sustain pedal on and off. In the original scheme of things, the second data byte in the message has a value of 0 to switch a control on, or 127 to switch it off, and no other data values are valid. Any message having a data byte value in the range 1 to 126 would therefore be ignored by any MIDI device which should happen to receive it. This has now been changed slightly, and values from 0 to 63 should be recognised as "off", while values from 64 to 127 should be recognised as "on".

Table 1.1

MIDI control no.	MSB control no.	LSB control no.
0	0	32
1	1	33
2	2	34
3	3	35
4	4	36
5	5	37
27	27	59
28	28	60
29	29	61
30	30	62
31	31	63

Global control

There is a little known provision in the MIDI specification that allows all the voices of a mode 4 device to be altered using a single control change message. This is known as a global control change message. Global control is achieved by sending the control change message on the channel one below the instrument's base channel. For example, if an instrument is operating in mode 4 on channels 4 to 11, the base channel is channel 4. Sending a control change message on channel 3 will result in that message affecting all eight channels from 4 to 11, provided this facility is included in the instrument's MIDI implementation. If the base channel is channel 1, then channel 16 becomes the global channel.

Standard controller assignments

As pointed out previously, there are now standard assignments for the MIDI controls. Although some older instruments might not conform to these assignments, any modern MIDI equipped instrument should do so. Table 1.2 gives a full list of the current MIDI control assignments. As will be apparent from this list, many of the controls are not currently assigned any specific function.

Table 1.2

Control no	Function
0	Undefined
1	Modulation wheel
2	Breath controller
3	Undefined
4	Foot pedal
5	Portamento time
6	Data entry MSB
7	Main volume control
8	Balance
9	Undefined
10	Pan
11	Expression controller
12-15	Undefined
16-19	General purpose controls
20-31	Undefined
32-63	LSB for controls 0 to 31
64	Sustain pedal
65	Portamento
66	Sostenuto
67	Soft pedal
68	Undefined
69	Hold 2
70-79	Undefined
80-83	General purpose controls
84-90	Undefined
91	External effects depth
92	Tremolo depth
93	Chorus depth

Control no	Function
94	Celeste depth
95	Phase depth
96	Data entry increment
97	Data entry decrement
98	Non-registered parameter MSB
99	Non-registered parameter LSB
100	Registered parameter MSB
101	Registered parameter LSB
102-120	Undefined
121-127	Channel mode messages

The degree to which MIDI controls are used varies enormously from one item of equipment to another. Some permit control of virtually every parameter via MIDI controls, while others provide control of only a few basic functions. With some instruments it is possible to assign each control to the desired MIDI control number. In order to use MIDI controls it may be necessary to do some careful reading of MIDI implementation charts etc. in equipment manuals. Due to the general nature of MIDI controls, there is always a strong possibility that several units will be to some extent incompatible, and may not be capable of operating together in the desired fashion. Although MIDI controls have great potential, a lack of true standardisation has perhaps led to them being less used than one might expect.

Parameters

Under the current scheme of things the MIDI controls are not used to directly control sound generator parameters such as the envelope shape attack time and filter cutoff frequency. They are mainly intended for general control of volume, effects, etc. It is permissible to control the sound generator circuits, but only in a slightly indirect manner. This is the purpose of controls 98 to 101, and 6/38. There are two types of parameter, which are the registered and non-registered varieties. The registered parameters are standardised, and are the same on all instruments that implement them. The non-registered parameters are not standardised, and their functions are likely to be completely different from one instrument to another.

It is obviously desirable if the parameters are, as far as possible, standardised. In practice it is not possible to achieve more than a very limited degree of standardisation due to the fact that modern instruments use several totally different methods of synthesis. Consequently, these are the only registered parameters currently in use.

Table 1.3

Parameter no.	Function
0	Pitch bend sensitivity
1	Fine tuning
2	Coarse tuning
3	Change tuning program
4	Change tuning bank

In order to alter the value of either type of parameter the required parameter number is first written to controls 98/99 or 100/101, as appropriate. This gives 14 bit resolution, which means that up to 16384 different controls can be used. This should be more than adequate, bearing in mind that this is the maximum number of controls per channel/voice of the instrument. Once a control has been selected the new value is written to controls 6 and 38. If no more than seven bit resolution is required, only control 6 needs to be used. Where more than seven bit resolution is used, and only one byte needs to be changed, it is recommended that fresh data should be sent to both controls. This is because the receiving device has no way of knowing whether to expect one or two bytes. Sending both bytes ensures that it is not left waiting for a second byte that will never be received. The receiving device should respond properly if only one byte is received, and should not wait indefinitely before altering the parameter.

There is an alternative to writing the new parameter value to controls 6 and 38. This is to either increment the parameter's value by an amount written to control 96, or decrement it by an amount written to control 97. This method could be useful when making frequent but minor alterations to parameters.

It is not safe to assume that an instrument or other MIDI device can be controlled via non-registered parameters. There are certainly plenty of instruments that can be controlled in this way, but there seems to be a trend towards the use of system exclusive messages instead. On the face of it this is an undesirable trend, since control via system exclusive messages really requires the use of a dedicated control unit or a computer running a dedicated control program. Although control change messages can be generated by a general purpose control unit or computer program, it would probably not be practical to make extensive use of non-registered parameters without some form of dedicated control unit or program. There is no standardisation using either of these routes to the sound generator circuits.

Mode changing etc.

A number of MIDI control numbers at the top end of the range are not used as ordinary controls. These are either not yet assigned to any particular purpose, or are used for functions such as MIDI mode changes. This is a list of the control numbers that have been assigned mode changing and similar functions.

Control no.	Function	Data
121	Reset all controls	Always 0
122	Local control	0 = off, 127 = on
123	All notes off	Always 0
124	Omni off	Always 0
125	Omni on	Always 0
126	Mono on	Number of channels
127	Mono off	Always 0

Control number 121, reset all controls, is one that has only been assigned its function relatively recently. Consequently, there are many instruments currently in circulation that do not recognise this message.

Local control

Local control enables an instrument's normal method of manual control to be switched off. What this usually means in practice is that the keyboard can be switched off. Obviously there are MIDI instruments other than keyboard types, and "local off" could mean deactivating some other means of local control (a wind type controller for instance). This message is obviously inapplicable to something like a MIDI expander which can only be controlled via its MIDI interface. Strictly speaking, this message does not switch off the keyboard or other means of local control. What it does is to disconnect it from the sound generator circuits. Any notes played on the keyboard will generate the appropriate messages at the MIDI output, and messages received at the MIDI input will be passed through to the sound generator circuits in the normal way. In effect the unit is converted into a separate MIDI keyboard and sound generator module. This might seem to be pointless, but it does increase the versatility of an instrument, and does have its uses. On the other hand, it is a feature that you may never get around to using!

The all notes off instruction is not intended as a normal means of switching off notes. It seems to be more intended as a way of getting all the notes silenced in the event of a failure which leaves notes sounding, such as can easily happen if a MIDI cable becomes damaged or accidentally disconnected mid-performance.

The mode change messages do not work on the basis of specific messages to select mode 1, mode 2, etc. Instead, the required mode is selected by switching omni and mono on or off. Remember here, that turning mono on switches poly off, and switching mono off turns poly on. For example, switching omni off and mono off selects mode 3 (omni off/poly). If you think in terms of the new mode names rather than the old names or mode numbers, selecting the omni and mono combinations is pretty straightforward. Note that when switching mono on, the second data byte in the message is not a dummy type having a value of zero. Instead, it is a value which sets the number of channels to be used in mono mode. As an example, if the base channel is channel 3, and six channels are set to mono mode, the instrument will occupy channels 3 to 8. In practice a data value of 0 is often used, and this simply sets all available channels to mono operation.

This covers all the channel messages and their variations. Next we will consider the system messages.

System messages (1111 - 240)

System messages all have the same code in the most significant nibble of the header byte, as indicated above. The least significant nibble is not needed for a channel number, and is used to indicate the type of system message. There are 16 code numbers available, but several of these have not yet been assigned a function. The following sections list all the system messages. The two numbers in each heading are the binary code, and the decimal equivalent (respectively). The binary numbers are only for the least significant nibble. The full binary code for the message is obtained by simply adding 1111 ahead of the four bit binary code provided. The decimal values are for the entire header byte, including the system message nibble.

Start system exclusive (0000 - 240), end system exclusive (0111 - 247)

In order to be successful MIDI had to lay down quite rigid standards so that good compatibility would be guaranteed between any two MIDI equipped devices that could reasonably be expected to operate properly together. MIDI had to end all the problems of incompatibility between units from different manufacturers that made life so difficult in the pre MIDI era when gate/CV interfacing was used. On the other hand, there was no point in laying down such a rigid standard that it prevented manufacturers from implementing imaginative new features in their equipment. If MIDI was made so rigid that it stifled instrument development, it would not be adopted by the equipment manufacturers.

The primary solution to these conflicting interests came in the form of system exclusive messages. A message of this type consists first of the "start system exclusive" header byte. This is followed by the manufacturer's identification code number. Next there are as many bytes as the equipment manufacturer sees fit to use. The precise manner in which information is coded into these data bytes is entirely at the discretion of the equipment manufacturer. This makes it possible to implement practically any feature imaginable via system exclusive messages. The manufacturer's code number acts as a key which ensures that only equipment which will respond to the message correctly will actually try to interpret it.

If a piece of equipment is fed with a system exclusive message which has the wrong manufacturer's identification code, it will simply ignore that message. This is absolutely essential, since the same set of data will mean something completely different to each instrument it is fed to, if they are all from different companies. If an instrument was allowed to respond to system exclusive messages for an instrument from another manufacturer, it could potentially do something drastic, such as completely scrambling all the parameters in the instrument's memory bank!

The final byte of data in a system exclusive message is followed by the "end system exclusive" message byte. This indicates to the devices receiving the message that the message has ended, and that normal MIDI operation has been resumed. When the system exclusive data bytes are being sent, like the data bytes in ordinary MIDI messages, they must be in the range 0 to 127. This ensures that this data can not be misinterpreted as message header bytes in general, and the system exclusive end message byte in particular.

This is a partial list of manufacturer's system exclusive identification numbers. The number of manufacturers' ID numbers now allocated is so large that one byte can not accommodate them all. Consequently, some manufacturers' ID codes are now three bytes long. The first byte in the group of three always has a value of 0, and this is followed by a two byte identification code.

Manufacturer	Hexadecimal	Decimal
SCI	01	1
Big Briar	02	2
Octave/Plateau	03	3
Moog	04	4
Passport Designs	05	5
Lexicon	06	6
Kurzweil	07	7
Fender	08	8
Ensoniq	0F	15
Oberheim	10	16
Apple Computer	11	17
Lowry	16	22
Emu Systems	18	24
Eventide	1C	28
Clarity	1F	31
Passac	20	32

Manufacturer	Hexadecimal	Decimal
SIEL	21	33
Hohner	24	36
PPG	29	41
JEN	2A	42
Elka/General Music	2F	47
Dynacord	30	48
Clavia Digital Instruments	33	51
Soundcraft Electronics	39	57
Waldorf Electronics Gmbh	3E	62
Kawai	40	64
Roland	41	65
Korg	42	66
Yamaha	43	67
Casio	44	68
Akai	47	71
Japan Victor	48	72
Sony	4C	76
TEAC Corp.	4E	78
Matsushita Electric	50	80
Fostex	51	81
Digital Music Corp	00 00 07	0 0 7
Alesis	00 00 0E	0 0 14
Opcode	00 00 16	0 0 22
Spatial Sound	00 00 18	0 0 24
CAE	00 00 26	0 0 38
Orban	00 00 21	0 0 33
Musonix	00 00 64	0 0 100

System exclusive messages are an increasingly important aspect of MIDI. Virtually all modern instruments seem able to make use of them in some way or other. This is a topic which is considered in some detail in a later chapter.

MTC quarter frame (0001 - 241)

MTC (MIDI time code) is a relatively recent addition to the MIDI standard. It is an involved subject, and an in-depth discussion of it here would be out of place. The basic purpose of MTC is to make it easier to keep a MIDI system synchronised with other equipment, particularly audio/visual equipment which uses SMPTE synchronisation. An MTC message is actually an eight byte sequence that provides a time in hours, minutes, seconds, and frames. MTC is considered in more detail in the chapter which deals with synchronisation.

Song position (0010 - 242)

In this context the word "song" really means a sequence, and this message would perhaps be more aptly named if it was called "sequence position". This is a three byte message which has the header byte followed by two data bytes. The data bytes are first the seven least significant bits of a 14 bit value, and then the seven most significant bits. This gives a data range of 0 to 16383. The purpose of this message is to set two sequencers to the same position in a sequence. The modern trend, and the one I certainly prefer, is to have everything under the control of one comprehensive sequencer, rather than having one or more units in the system under the control of their own "personal" sequencers. However, the use of instruments under the control of their own sequencers, especially drum machines, is a well established and still much used technique.

The idea is that MIDI sequencers should have a counter that registers the number of sixteenth beats since the beginning of the sequence. If one sequencer sends out a song position pointer message, then any others in the system should set their counters to the value contained in the message, so that they are all set to the same point in the sequence. A resolution of sixteenth beats gives good accuracy, but with a maximum count of 16384 it means that sequences are limited to no more than 1024 beats in length. This feature provides a very quick and easy means of setting two or more sequencers to the same point in a sequence, and as such it is very useful. It is not implemented by all sequencers, but it seems to be a well supported MIDI feature. One point worth bearing in mind is that some sequencers are much quicker at adjusting to new positions in a sequence than are others. If a sequence is restarted very soon after a song position message has been sent there is the possibility that one sequencer will not start immediately, causing a lack of synchronisation.

Song select (0011 - 243)

This is a two byte message which consists of the header byte followed by a data byte which contains the song number to be selected. Again, the word "song" means a sequence, and this is a means of switching from one sequence to another. This MIDI message can accommodate up to 128 sequences, but most sequencers can handle far fewer than this. By no means all sequencers can handle more than one sequence. The most common use of this message is probably in a system having a main sequencer plus one or more drum machines having built-in sequencers. It enables the main sequencer to switch the drum machine or machines from one pattern to another.

Tune request (0110 - 246)

The name of this command suggests that its function is much the same as the song select instruction described previously. In fact the word "tune" in this context means tune in the sense of tuning an instrument. Some instruments have a built-in automatic tuning facility. When this is activated, via MIDI or the front panel controls, the tuning of the instrument is adjusted so that it accurately matches a built-in reference oscillator. This normally adjusts the instrument to the standard concert pitch which has middle A at a frequency of 440Hz. A tune request message will cause all the instruments in the system that support this feature to automatically retune themselves. No timing or pitch information is sent via MIDI, and the instruments are all tuned against their own internal reference oscillators. Despite the lack of a common reference source, the individual reference oscillators should be accurate enough to ensure that there are no significant pitch differences between the instruments in the system. As this message is one that merely activates an internal function of the instruments in the system, it does not carry any data and is a single byte instruction.

This message is one that is not recognised by many instruments. Modern types mostly have very accurate tuning that is controlled by a highly stable quartz crystal controlled oscillator. This gives no significant drift even over a long period of time. When MIDI was first devised there were still a great many analogue synthesisers being produced, and these did have a definite tendency to drift in pitch. They often had built-in tuning circuits. This feature is largely obsolete these days.

Clock signal (1000 - 248), start (1010 - 250), continue (1011 - 251), stop (1100 - 252)

The normal way of keeping two or more sequencers accurately synchronised is to have one sequencer send out a regular series of signals to all the other sequencers in the system. For drum machines and some other purposes this used to be a series of simple electronic pulses, but these days the synchronisation is normally provided via a MIDI link. Each pulse is replaced by a single byte MIDI message - the MIDI clock message. These messages are sent at the rate of twenty four per crotchet (quarter note). The MIDI clock system radically differs from the old pulse system in that sequences are not started and stopped by starting and stopping the clock signals. Instead, there are specific messages to start and halt a sequence, and the clock signal is a continuous type. It is not actually essential for the clock signal to be running all the time, and if desired it can commence after a start message, and cease after a stop message. This is up to the equipment and software designers.

In addition to the stop and start messages there is a continue type. This starts a sequence, but it takes up where it left off. With the start message, the sequence is always started from the beginning, even if it was halted half way through by a stop message. Apart from starting a sequence at the point where it was halted, a continue message can also be used after a song position pointer type. This causes the sequence to start at the point indicated by the song position pointer message. The original MIDI clock system incidentally, operated in a slightly different manner to the one described here. Few devices using the old system were ever made, and it can now be regarded as totally obsolete.

These four messages are all single byte types. They are sometimes called system real-time messages. Accurate timing of these messages is essential, since any lack of accuracy in this respect will be reflected in rather ragged timing of the sequence being played. The MIDI standard actually allows these messages to be sent in the middle of other messages, so that really accurate timing can be achieved. These messages can not interrupt another message mid-byte, but can be placed within bytes of another message. Because the most significant bit of a message header byte is always 1, but it is 0 for data bytes, it is easy for designers to produce equipment that can sort out system real-time messages that appear within another message.

MIDI timing signals are not recognised by many instruments and other MIDI devices, since they lack any form of built-in sequencer. Modern instruments which have a built-in sequencer can send MIDI clock signals or synchronise properly to any that are received. With many early MIDI instruments there is a less than full implementation of MIDI synchronisation. Many have sequencers that can either send clock signals or respond to them, but do not have both features. As always, it is worth carefully checking MIDI implementation charts, especially when using an older instrument.

Active sensing (1110 - 254)

This is a feature that seemed to be dying out, but which has made something of a comeback in some recent instruments. It is one that is potentially very useful, but far from essential. The idea is for the MIDI controller to send this single byte message at less than 300 millisecond (0.3 second) intervals if there is no other MIDI activity. If a MIDI instrument fails to receive an active sensing message or any other MIDI message after more than 300 milliseconds has elapsed, it knows that there is a fault somewhere in the system, and it silences all its sound generator circuits. This avoids the possibility of having notes left droning if there is a fault, or if there is a mishap such as someone tripping over and breaking a MIDI cable.

Active sensing is an optional feature, and one that few instruments have actually implemented. Where an instrument does support this feature, it will not be activated until the instrument has received an initial active sensing message. Although it might seem that using active sensing unnecessarily increases MIDI activity, thus increasing the risk of MIDI choke, this is not actually the case. Remember that an active sensing message needs to be sent only if there is no other MIDI activity. Consequently, they are sent only at times when there is absolutely no risk of MIDI choke occurring. With the messages sent at intervals of only a little under 300 milliseconds, there are too few of them to significantly affect MIDI choke problems anyway.

System reset (1111 - 255)

This is another single byte message. Its effect is to take the instrument back to its default settings. This means taking it back to its switch-on state. Not all instruments implement this feature, and in many cases it would be pointless. With a disk based instrument such as a sound sampler for instance, the unit can not produce any sounds in the start up state. It must first have some data loaded from disk. I suppose that with some instruments this message could be useful. If the control settings should all become scrambled for some reason (such as someone leaning on them or if there is a MIDI error!), then this message might provide a quick way back to normality.

This is the full set of MIDI messages as things stand at present. There are proposals to make use of currently unassigned MIDI codes. There is also a possibility of minor changes to existing codes, although anything more than a few minor changes to little used codes seems highly unlikely. With MIDI having established a firm standard that enables a wide range of units from numerous manufacturers to all work efficiently in the same system, no one is likely to make any alterations that might jeopardise this situation. Anyway, at the time of writing this there are nothing more than proposals under consideration, and this is the current extent of MIDI.

The final section of this chapter is a set of tables plus some brief notes of explanation that provide details of the MIDI codes. This should be useful for quick reference purposes.

Channel voice codes

All the channel code messages have the most significant bit of the header byte set to 1, and the least significant nibble carrying the MIDI channel value. Remember that the value used to select a channel is one less than the channel number, because the channels are numbered 1 to 16, but they are selected by values from 0 to 15. With three bits available to specify the type of message, a maximum of eight messages can be accommodated. In fact there are only seven channel message codes, as the eighth code is used for system messages. This table gives details of the binary and decimal values used to select each channel voice message

Channel voice message

Message	Binary	Decimal	No. of data bytes
Note off	1000cccc	128	2
Note on	1001cccc	144	2
Poly key pressure	1010cccc	160	2
Control change	1011cccc	176	2
Program change	1100cccc	192	1
Overall key pressure	1101cccc	208	1
Pitch wheel	1110cccc	224	2

In the binary column, "cccc" represents the bits that carry the channel value. In terms of the decimal number that must be sent to the MIDI port, take the value in the "decimal" column, add the channel number to it, and deduct one. For example, a "note on" message on channel 8 would require a value of 151 (144 + 8 = 152, 152 - 1 = 151). Remember that a "note on" instruction having a velocity value of 0 can be used as a "note off" instruction.

The table shown below gives the functions of the data bytes for the channel voice messages. All data bytes are in the range 0 to 127.

Message	Byte 1	Byte 2
Note off	Note value	Velocity value
Note on	Note value	Velocity value
Poly key pressure	Note value	Pressure value
Control change	Control number	New control value
Program change	Program number	
Overall key pressure	Pressure value	
Pitch wheel	Least significant byte	Most significant byte

With the pitch wheel message the two data bytes are combined to give a single fourteen bit number. The true value sent is therefore obtained by multiplying the first byte by 128 and then adding it to the second data byte. For instance, data bytes of 28 and 79 provide a pitch wheel value of 3663 (28 x 128 = 3584, 3584 + 79 = 3663). A value of 8192 (data bytes of 64 and 0) provides zero pitch change. As explained previously, the same system can be used with the variable controls, by pairing them so as to give two data bytes. For controls that only give an on/off action (i.e. controls 64 to 95) only values of 0 ("off") and 127 ("on") are valid, and other values will be ignored. Note that the controls are numbered from 0 to 127, and not 1 to 128. Therefore, unlike selecting a channel, the value actually used is the same as the control number.

Channel mode messages

Channel mode messages use the same header code as the control change message, and are accessed with a first data byte having a value between 121 and 127. Details of the channel mode messages are provided in the next table.

Control no.	Function	Data byte
121	Reset all controls	Always 0
122	Local control	0 = off, 127 = on
123	All notes off	Always 0
124	Omni mode off	Always 0
125	Omni mode on	Always 0
126	Mono mode on	Number of channels, or 0 to use all channels
127	Poly mode on	Always 0

Obviously, when the mono mode is switched on, the poly mode is switched off, and vice versa. A mode change switches off all notes, but switching local control on or off or using the reset all controls message does not. This feature, and the separate "all notes off" instruction, should be considered as a safety net feature to prevent notes being accidentally left switched on, and not an alternative to the normal "note off" message. In fact it does not seem to be a requirement that MIDI equipment actually responds to any form of "all notes off" instruction, and many instruments ignore this instruction. This next table shows the controllers that must be written to in order to obtain each of the four standard MIDI modes.

Mode 1 (omni on/poly)	125 and 127
Mode 2 (omni on/mono)	125 and 126
Mode 3 (omni off/poly)	124 and 127
Mode 4 (omni off/mono)	124 and 126

In order to be certain of selecting any MIDI mode, the appropriate two controllers must be activated. Remember that the "mono on" message must include (in the second data byte) the number of channels to be used in the mono mode, or a value of 0 if all channels are to be used in this mode.

System messages

The system real-time messages all consist of a single byte with the most significant nibble set at 1111 (240 in decimal). Some other system messages do include a data byte or bytes, but they also have all bits in the most significant nibble set to 1. The least significant nibble is not required for channel identification purposes, and these four bits are used to identify the instruction. This gives a maximum of sixteen different system messages. The binary and decimal values needed for the system real-time messages are listed below:

Binary	Decimal	Message type
11111000	248	Clock signal
11111001	249	Undefined
11111010	250	Start
11111011	251	Continue
11111100	252	Stop
11111101	253	Undefined
11111110	254	Active sensing
11111111	255	System reset

These system real-time messages can be sent at any time, even in the middle of other messages. The system reset instruction must not be sent at switch-on, or when equipment is reset. This could easily result in the system hanging up with reset messages being circulated indefinitely! The clock signals are send at a rate of twenty four per quarter note. Active sensing is optional (and little used in current MIDI equipment). Because it is optional, receiving equipment will not automatically switch off all notes in its absence. Equipment that does implement this feature will switch off all notes only after at least one active sensing byte has been received, and there has then been a gap of more than 300 milliseconds since the last message of this type was received.

System common messages

Message	Binary	Decimal	Data bytes
Start system excl.	11110000	240	Maker's code/etc.
MTC quarter frame	11110001	241	Values
Song position	11110010	242	LS byte/MS byte
Song select	11110011	243	Song no.
Undefined	11110100	244	-
Undefined	11110101	245	-
Tune request	11110110	246	None
End system excl.	11110111	247	None

The "song select" status byte is followed by a single data byte which is the song number, and is from 0 to 127. This selects the sequence that will be played when a system real-time "start" message is received by the sequencer. The song pointer status byte is followed by two data bytes which are combined to give a 14 bit number (with the least significant byte being sent first). This can be used to set the sequencer to a certain point in the selected sequence. Some codes in this category are, as yet, undefined. The system exclusive instructions have been included in this list so that they are available for quick reference purposes, but they are not strictly speaking system common messages.

MIDI routing

Even if a MIDI system has only two or three units, there are likely to be a few options when it comes to choosing a method of connecting everything together. With more complex systems having half a dozen or more MIDI devices there are likely to be numerous permutations available. In many cases it will not be necessary to opt for anything more than one of the basic methods of wiring together a MIDI system, but it is as well to know what options are available to you. You might not ever need one of the more elaborate setups, but an unusual configuration might at some time be the answer to an awkward situation. In this chapter we will consider systems from the most basic setups through to some of the more unusual, but potentially useful systems.

Chaining reaction

The most basic method of MIDI interconnection is the chain type. This basic scheme of things is illustrated in Figure 2.1. The output of the controller, which in this case is a keyboard instrument, is coupled to the input of a second keyboard instrument. The THRU socket of this second instrument is coupled to the input of an expander, which in turn has its THRU socket connected to the input of another expander. In theory at any rate, you can go on chaining together as many MIDI devices as you like, with the THRU socket of one unit connecting through to the MIDI input of the next unit. The signal at a THRU input is a replica of the signal fed to the input socket, and so this method of interconnection results in the signal from the controller being carried down the chain from one device to the next.

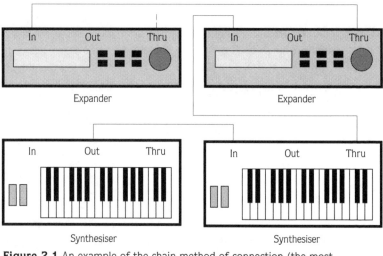

Figure 2.1 An example of the chain method of connection (the most common system of MIDI interconnection)

A point in favour of the chain method of connection is that it does not require the use of any additional hardware. Provided the MIDI units are fitted with THRU sockets, you can simply wire together as many units as you have. In practice, not all MIDI units actually have a THRU socket, and this method of interconnection is not always possible. As explained previously, MIDI lays down a framework to which MIDI devices must conform, but it does not lay down much in the way of minimum requirements. The lack of a THRU socket is a pretty glaring omission, but one that is permissible within the MIDI standard. At one time many instruments, especially keyboard types, lacked a THRU socket. Fortunately, things have improved in recent years, and it is likely that all MIDI devices now include this facility. If only one unit in the system lacks a THRU socket, then there is no problem. This unit is used as the last one in the chain. If more than one unit lacks a THRU socket, then the chain method of interconnection can not be used.

Delays

Although in theory it is possible to connect together any number of MIDI units in a chained system, and the MIDI standard does not specify a maximum figure for the number of units that can be wired up in this way, in practice there might be a definite limit on the number of units that can be chained together successfully. The problem here is one that has become known as MIDI "delay". This is a somewhat misunderstood problem, and many MIDI users seem to be under the impression that the problem is simply one of a cumulative delay through the system causing instruments at the end of the chain to lag behind those at the beginning, giving poor timing of notes. This may sound quite plausible, but if you study the MIDI hardware specification it becomes apparent that this is not possible.

At each MIDI input there is a device called an opto-isolator. This is basically just a light emitting diode (l.e.d.) having its output directed at a photocell, with the two components contained in an opaque case. The MIDI signal pulses the l.e.d. on and off, which in turn switches the photocell on and off. This couples the input signal through the opto-isolator, and on into the main electronics of the unit. This might seem like an unnecessarily complicated way of doing things, but there is a big advantage in this method. There is no direct electrical connection between one MIDI unit and the next. This can help to avoid problems with such things as noise from digital circuits being coupled into the audio signal path, "hum" loops (or "earth" loops as they are also know), and the damage that can occur due to high voltages when two mains powered units which do not have earthed chassis are connected together.

The signal for the THRU socket is normally taken from the output side of the opto-isolator. In electronic terms opto-isolators, even the better ones, are not particularly fast components. However, in human terms they are very fast, and any delay through opto-isolator of adequate quality for MIDI use is likely to be no more than a few microseconds. In other words, no more than a few millionths of a second. On testing several instruments from different manufacturers I have never been able to measure a delay significantly greater than this. Even with an accumulated delay through a few dozen opto-isolators, we are only talking in terms of a total delay of a millisecond or so (i.e. about a thousandth of a second or so).

This is totally insignificant when compared to other likely delays in the system, and is not long enough to be perceptible to the human ear. When dealing with delays it is a good idea to bear in mind that one instrument being played just a metre further away from the listener than another instrument will introduce a delay of approximately three milliseconds. If all the players in an orchestra were to play in perfect unison, no one in the audience would actually hear it as such! You can not perceive extremely small timing errors, and it would ruin your musical enjoyment if you could.

It is likely that so-called MIDI delays are actually the result of MIDI choke. This is a subject that is pursued in a later chapter, and we will not consider it in any great detail here. It is basically a problem of MIDI sometimes being unable to cope with the flow of messages at times of very high activity. In a severe case it results in messages being missed out, or only some bytes being sent, with the system effectively crashing out of control as a result. More usually there are no missed or corrupted messages, but some are delayed while the controller works through the backlog of messages as fast as the MIDI interface will take them. I think it is true to say that problems of this type are often not due to MIDI not being able to send the data at a high enough rate. The microprocessor in the MIDI controller may be the limiting factor on what the system can handle when large amounts of data are being processed. Either way, the problem of ragged timing is not due to the chain method of connection. It will happen whatever method of inter-connection is used.

Smearing

The real MIDI delay problem is one of the signal being degraded slightly as it goes through each opto-isolator. Strictly speaking it is not a delay through the opto-isolator that causes a problem, but what is termed its slew-rate. Ideally the output signal should switch instantly from one logic level to the other. In practice no electronic circuit can achieve this, and opto-isolators are far from being the fastest of components.

Figure 2.2 shows how the cumulative slowing down of the transition from one logic level to the other can cause a massive degradation in the signal quality. This could result in units more than so far along the chain failing to receive a signal of usable quality, with them either

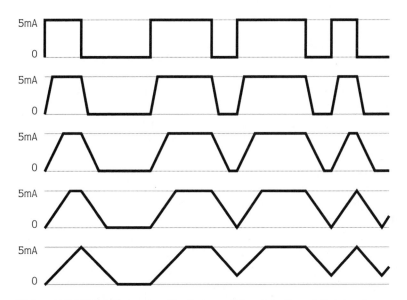

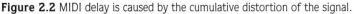

Figure 2.2 MIDI delay is caused by the cumulative distortion of the signal.

tending to decode data incorrectly, or to simply ignore some messages as a result. In reality it would probably take quite a long chain of instruments to produce a substantial degradation of the signal. On the other hand, the MIDI instruments I have tested seem to require a very good quality input signal if they are to operate reliably. A slowing down of the input signal that is barely perceptible when the signal is viewed using an oscilloscope seems to be sufficient to produce a "MIDI ERROR" message on the display of many instruments.

There is probably no major risk of MIDI delays producing problems with a system consisting of about half a dozen or less MIDI units. For those fortunate enough to have more than about half a dozen MIDI units in their music systems it might be as well not to use the chain system of connection.

Star system

The alternative to the chain method of connection is the star type. This relies on the MIDI controller having several output sockets, but very few have more than a single MIDI output. The way around this problem is to use a THRU box, which is simply a device that has an input socket plus about four or more THRU outputs. Figure 2.3 shows the way in which a THRU box is used. The input signal from the MIDI controller is replicated at each of the THRU sockets. Each unit in the system is fed from a THRU socket, and therefore receives the signal from the controller. This avoids problems with MIDI delays since each unit receives a signal that has previously gone through just a single opto-isolator (i.e. the one in the THRU box). The only real drawback of this system is that it will often involve the additional expense of the THRU box and an extra MIDI cable. Probably the best course of action in most cases is to first try the chain method of connection, and to bother with the star system only if problems are experienced with the chain setup.

It is not essential to rigidly adhere to either the chain system or the star type. Any method of connection that results in the signal from the controller getting through to each unit in the system should give satis-factory results. A combination of the two methods should be perfectly satisfactory, as in the example system of Figure 2.4. Here the MIDI con-troller has two output sockets, with each one feeding a simple two unit chain system. With a very large system a combination of the star and chain methods of connection might offer the most practical solution.

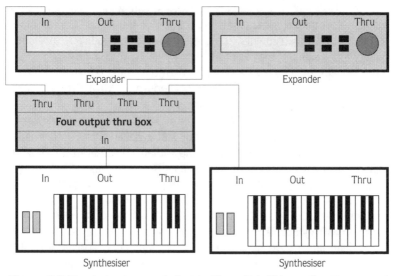

Figure 2.3 The star system equivalent to Figure 2.1. This requires the addition of a THRU box.

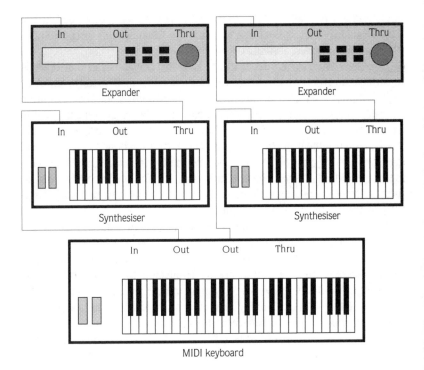

Figure 2.4 A combination of the star and chain systems is sometimes the best option.

Sequencing

In the systems described so far there has been a keyboard instrument as the controller, with a number of instruments slaved to it. MIDI can be used to good effect in this manner, but most systems probably go beyond a simple slaving setup. MIDI is much used in real-time sequencing using what is often a computer based sequencer. This application requires that sequences should be played into the computer via what is usually a MIDI keyboard (but which could also be drum pads, a MIDI guitar, etc.), and that the computer should send completed sequences to the instruments in the system. A typical setup of this type would have the computer, a keyboard instrument, and a couple of rack-mount instruments connected as shown in Figure 2.5. This uses the chain method of connection, but the star system alternative of

Figure 2.6 gives exactly the same result. The systems described in the rest of this chapter will all make use of the chain system of connection, but they all have star system equivalents.

This setup differs from those discussed previously in that there is a connection from the output of the keyboard instrument to the input of the computer, as well as the main chain system from the computer through the various instruments. A point that should be kept in mind is that a MIDI system can normally have just one controller. In this case there would appear to be two controllers (the keyboard and the computer). This is indeed the case, but we have what are effectively two separate MIDI systems. There is the main system which consists of the computer plus all the instruments, and a secondary system comprised of just the keyboard and the computer.

In use you would either play sequences into the computer via the keyboard, or play completed sequences back into the instruments, so that only one controller would be in use at any one time. There are no problems with two outputs being connected together, and even if the computer and the keyboard should output signals simultaneously, this will not cause any conflicts. Incidentally, MIDI outputs (including THRU types) include current limiting resistors that should avoid any damage if two sockets of this type should be accidentally connected together. No damage should occur, but connecting two outputs together will not do anything worthwhile either.

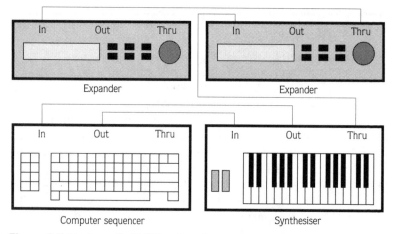

Figure 2.5 Most practical MIDI systems have two controllers in an arrangement of this type.

Local off

With a system of the type shown in Figure 2.6 there is the option of using the keyboard instrument with or without local control switched off. The best method depends on the particular equipment you are using, and is to some extent a matter of personal preference. With local control left on, anything you play onto the keyboard will be produced by the synthesizer. However, you will often be playing parts that should be played on other instruments in the system. It might be that the keyboard instrument can be set to provide a suitable substitute sound, so that you at least get a good idea of what the played-back track will sound like when it is produced by the right instrument. If the keyboard instrument can not provide a reasonable substitute, it might be the case that you can play the track properly anyway, with either the wrong sound or even just the clatter of the keyboard! I find this type of thing impossible, but apparently some people can manage it without too much difficulty.

A much better alternative is to have some means of directing the keyboard's output to both the sequencer and the appropriate instrument. By far the easiest way of doing this is to use a sequencer

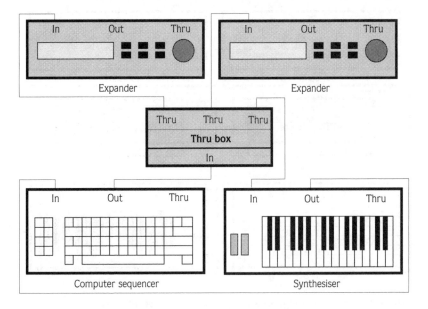

Figure 2.6 The star connection equivalent to the system of Figure 2.5.

that has a "THRU" facility. This is a very simple but invaluable feature, and all it does is to transmit from the OUT socket any messages that are received at the input. Remember that the input signal is normally reproduced at the THRU socket and not the OUT type. With the THRU facility turned on, a track played into the sequencer will be coupled through to all the instruments. It is then just a matter of making sure that the keyboard is transmitting on the right channel for the particular voice and instrument concerned. Fortunately most modern keyboard instruments can be easily adjusted to transmit on any desired MIDI channel. With a keyboard that operates only on channel 1 it could be advantageous to feed its output to the sequencer via a channeliser, so that the desired channel could be selected via this add-on. Alternatively, the sequencer might have the ability to switch the output signal to any desired channel.

One slightly disappointing feature of many THRU facilities is that they operate only when a sequence is being recorded. This can make it a bit difficult to check that the instrument which must reproduce a track is set to the right sound, and set up correctly in all respects, prior

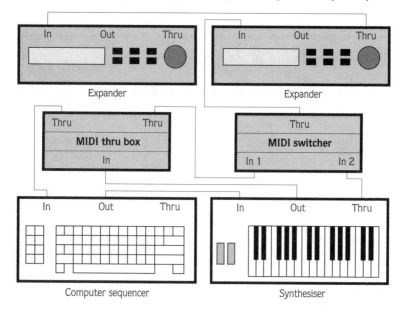

Figure 2.7 A hardware method of obtaining switching from computer to keyboard control.

to recording a track. One way around this is to record a dummy track while setting things up, and to delete it as soon as you have everything just right. Alternatively, the sequencer may well have some facility that enables notes to be easily sent on the desired channel for general testing and setting up purposes. As always, you will need to carefully read the instruction manuals for your MIDI equipment, and probably do some experimenting as well, in order to find out just what can and can not be achieved.

If the sequencer does not have a software solution to the problem in the form of a THRU facility, then a hardware solution must be sought. Probably the simplest method is to use a MIDI switcher, as shown in Figure 2.7. This has two inputs and a single THRU output. Only one input is coupled to the THRU output at any one time, and a switch is used to select which input this is. In fact some units provide automatic switching, which makes them very convenient in this sort of setup. A manual switcher is not difficult to build if you are reasonably competent with a small electric soldering iron. You just need a small case, a d.p.d.t. switch, and a couple of 5 way (180 degree) DIN sockets connected in the manner shown in Figure 2.8.

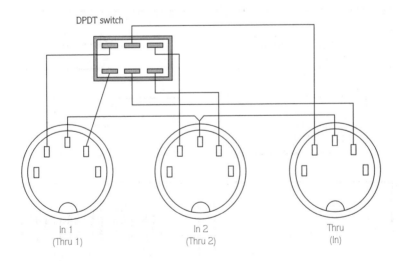

Figure 2.8 The wiring for a simple home constructed MIDI switcher.

Merging

As an alternative to a switcher, you could use a MIDI merge unit. This is a substantially more sophisticated device than a simple switching unit, and it will actually combine the outputs of two MIDI units to produce a proper output. If there are messages received on the two inputs simultaneously, it will couple one signal through to the output, while storing the other in its memory. When the first signal has stopped, it will recover the second signal from its memory and transmit it. These units can not be guaranteed to always function correctly, since with high activity on both inputs there could simply be too much data to send on one output. Eventually the unit's memory would become full, and messages would then be lost.

In practice this is not likely to occur, as it is unlikely that there would be high enough activity on both inputs for long enough to cause an overload. MIDI choke in a milder form, and a consequent loss of timing accuracy is a more realistic problem with these units. In the present context there is no possibility of choke occurring. A MIDI merge unit will give the desired effect, but it is a rather expensive solution to the problem. As there will only be messages received at one input or the other, it would really be functioning as nothing more than an automatic switcher.

If a manual switcher is used, when recording tracks this is used to connect the THRU socket of the sequencer to the instruments. When playing back a track or entire sequence, it is used to connect the OUT socket to the instruments.

True merging

Although a merge unit is over-specified for the example application just described, these devices do have their uses. As pointed out earlier in this chapter, you can not control a group of MIDI devices from two controllers simply by connecting the MIDI outputs of the controllers together and using them as if they were a single output. This might actually work provided the two units did not output messages simultaneously, but is not something I would suggest you try. With both units sending data at once there is no chance of this method, or any simple mixing process working properly. The messages from the two units would be scrambled together in such a way as to give any device receiving the combined signal no chance at all of unscrambling the signal and decoding the two sets of messages. A merge unit must ensure that the messages received at the inputs are transferred to the output socket as complete and entirely separate entities.

Using two controllers

In most situations a single controller is probably all that is required, and a merge unit will not be needed. There are situations where a unit of this type is essential though, and a simple switcher will not give the desired action. As an example, assume that a keyboard player wishes to play a synthesizer via a separate MIDI keyboard, and a percussionist wishes to use its percussion section via a MIDI drum pad. A modern instrument may well have enough voices to satisfy the requirements of both players, but it is only possible to connect the keyboard or the drum pad to the instrument's MIDI input. A merge unit used in the manner shown in Figure 2.9 provides a solution to the problem. Provided the keyboard, drum pad, and voices of the instrument can all be set to suitable MIDI channels, the drum pad and the keyboard can be made to produce the right sounds from the instrument.

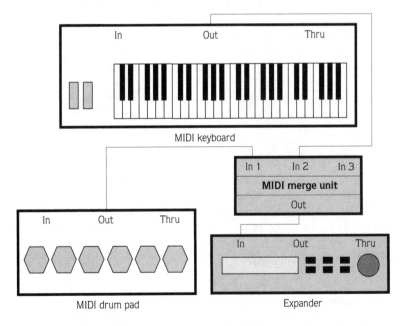

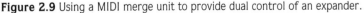
Figure 2.9 Using a MIDI merge unit to provide dual control of an expander.

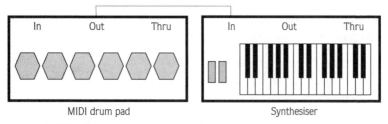

MIDI drum pad   Synthesiser

Figure 2.10 MIDI instruments can handle simultaneous local and external control, which permits this simple system to work properly.

Note that if the instrument had a built-in keyboard, it would not be necessary to set it to local off, and then use a merge unit to combine the output from the keyboard with the output of the drum pad. You could simply connect the drum pad to the MIDI input of the instrument, as in Figure 2.10. All the MIDI keyboard instruments I have encountered have been quite happy to operate with notes being played on the keyboard while MIDI messages were at the same time being fed to the MIDI input. You just need to be careful not to exceed the maximum number of notes the unit can play at once.

Using a merger with a sequencer

Perhaps a more likely use for a merge unit is in a sequencer system where tracks may be originated from a keyboard plus a drum pad, or perhaps some other form of MIDI controller such as a guitar, a wind type, or perhaps just another keyboard. Provided only one unit or the other would be used to play tracks, a MIDI switcher would suffice. Although at one time MIDI sequencers all seemed to restrict the user to recording one track at a time, the more sophisticated units now permit two or more tracks to be laid down at once. Recording one track at a time is not to everyone's liking, and a merge unit provides a means of recording two tracks simultaneously using two controllers. In fact some merge units have more than two inputs, and with a suitable sequencer would permit three (or possibly more) tracks to be recorded simultaneously. Figure 2.11 shows a typical sequencer setup having three controllers and a merge unit.

Using a merger with a MIDI pedal

Another use for merge units is when a MIDI pedal is used with a sequencer system. This could be something like an all notes off pedal, a multiple control pedal, or virtually any type of MIDI pedal in fact. You

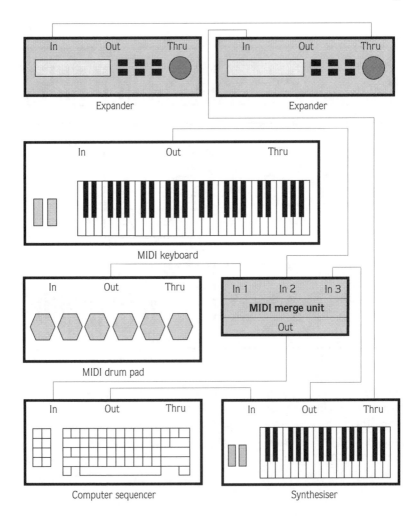

Figure 2.11 With this system, up to three devices can be used to simultaneously record tracks in the sequencer.

might wish to record information from the pedal into the sequencer while also playing on the keyboard, which would be allowed by the setup shown in Figure 2.12. Alternatively, you might wish to directly control the instruments in the system from the pedal, which could be achieved using the arrangement shown in Figure 2.13. If you need to

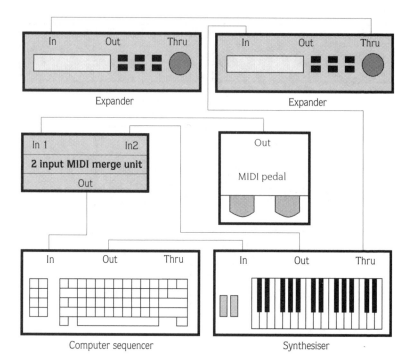

Figure 2.12 This arrangement permits the pedal to be used to add tracks primarily from the synthesizer's keyboard.

be able to use both systems, it is necessary to resort to some MIDI switchers, or to do a lot of unplugging and reconnecting. A major use of MIDI merge units is in systems that include a tape synchroniser unit. In fact some tape synchronisers actually include a built-in merge function. This is a topic which is covered in the chapter on synchronisation.

Patching it up

If you start to use complex setups which need frequent reconfiguring in order to obtain the desired effect, it would probably be worthwhile investing in a MIDI patchbay unit. MIDI patchbays vary enormously in their complexity and facilities. However simple or complex, their basic function is always to route signals around the system in the desired fashion. The usual arrangement is to have a number of inputs and outputs, and in a typical unit there would be something like eight of

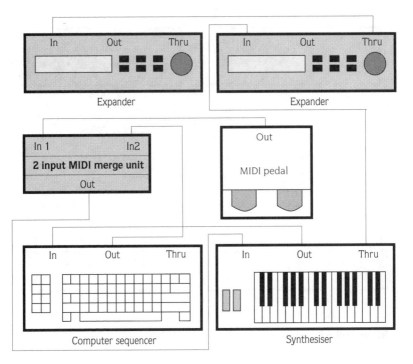

Figure 2.13 This setup enables the pedal to be used live with played-back sequences.

each type. As most MIDI systems have more controlled units than controllers (or units capable of acting as controllers), some patch bays have fewer "IN"s than "OUT"s.

The general idea is to connect the input and output of each MIDI unit in the system to the output and input sockets (respectively) of the MIDI patchbay unit. This gives a typical setup of the type shown in Figure 2.14. The THRU sockets of the units in the system are not normally required, and when using a patchbay you have what is really just a star system, but one that can be quickly and easily reconfigured. Probably the only situation in which it might be worthwhile connecting a THRU socket is in a sequencer system where the sequencer has a THRU facility. Using the THRU facility might sometimes reduce the amount of switch changing needed in order to reconfigure the system.

A simple manual patchbay has a number of switches that control which outputs each input connects to. By setting the appropriate

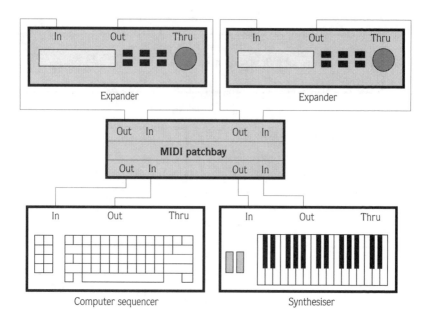

Figure 2.14 An example system using a MIDI patchbay. The patchbay is used to determine which INs connect to which OUTs.

switches to the on state, you can therefore connect any controller to any controlled devices. With many patchbays there is no proper merge facility, and you must be careful not to have more than one controller outputting messages at any one time. Having two controllers operating simultaneously should not cause any damage, but it is almost certain to cause a malfunction.

There is a slight drawback to simple patchbay units in that you may need to keep changing the settings of numerous switches as you move between one much used configuration and another. A typical sequencing setup is a good example of this. When recording sequences, the output of the keyboard would feed into the input of the sequencer. Depending on whether or not the sequencer has a THRU facility, the inputs of the instruments would be fed from the output of either the sequencer or the keyboard instrument. When playing back sequences, the connection from the keyboard to the sequencer could probably be left in place without any problems, and if the instruments were not already fed from the output of the sequencer, they would have to be switched so that they were. For each instrument or other controlled device in the system, this would involve closing one switch and opening another. If the sequencer had only a limited THRU facility, a similar amount of switch changing would be needed in order to permit the keyboard to control the instruments etc. in the system.

It can sometimes be made easier to change from one configuration to another if some of the connections are not taken via the patchbay. I would not advise this though, since it loses the main advantage of using a patchbay, which is the ability to quickly set up any desired configuration. As most patchbays are not particularly cheap, you need to give some thought as to how much use a unit of this type will really be. If you are only going to switch between two configurations, and will rarely (if ever) use any other setup, a MIDI switcher may offer a much cheaper and easier solution to the problem. The more MIDI units you have, and the greater the number of configurations you will use, the more worthwhile a patchbay should be. However, with a simple type there will inevitably be a large amount of switch changing, and it might be worthwhile making up patch charts showing the switch settings needed for the standard system configurations. This should aid rapid and error-free changes from one setup to another, especially in the early stages of using the patchbay unit.

Programmable patchbays

The more sophisticated patchbays make it easy to switch between standard configurations by having memory circuits that can store what is typically dozens of sets of interconnections. You can set up as many sets of interconnections as you are ever likely to need, and then recall any desired setup just by pressing two or three buttons. Units of this type, like most electronic musical instruments that have a memory facility for patch information, almost invariably have a battery back-up system for the memory circuit. The battery generally needs replacement only about every five years, but the unit may need to be returned to the dealer or a service centre in order to have a new battery fitted. The battery ensures that the data for your sets of interconnections is not lost when the unit is switched off at the end of each session. If you had to reprogram all the sets of interconnections at the beginning of each session, it would probably be easier to have a simple switch-type patchbay unit!

Program change vs system exclusive

MIDI control seems to be a standard feature of programmable patchbays. There are three basic ways in which such a unit can be controlled via MIDI. These are by way of system exclusive, controller, or program change messages. Control of patchbays is not necessarily limited to just one of these methods, and there might even be the option of all three. The use of MIDI controls for this type of thing seems to be strictly limited though, and is an option that is unlikely to be available to you. As MIDI does not have messages specifically for the control of patchbays, system exclusive messages are perhaps the obvious method of control. There is a drawback to their use in this context in that there is no way of using system exclusive messages unless you have some means of generating them. There are ways around this potential problem, see Chapter 8 on system exclusive matters.

Probably the main means of controlling patchbays via MIDI, and controlling many other MIDI gadgets such as audio mixers, audio signal routers, digital effects units, and MIDI processors, is to use program change messages. This operates on the basis of having each set of con-figuration data assigned to a MIDI program number. The advantage of program numbers is that they can be generated by many items of MIDI equipment, and are easily stored in sequencers along with other MIDI data. If you set a synthesizer to a new program number, it will usually transmit the appropriate program change message. Most pieces of equipment that make use of program change messages can generate them very easily. Even MIDI controller messages are not so easily gen-erated, unless you happen to own a suitable MIDI controller pedal.

System exclusive messages are easily generated provided the piece of equipment you wish to control has a facility for generating the appropriate messages. Remember that these messages are specific to one particular manufacturer, or quite possibly even to one item of equipment from one manufacturer. You are unlikely to be able to use a synthesizer to generate system exclusive messages to control a MIDI patchbay or some other MIDI gadget. There can sometimes be prob-lems if an attempt is made to store system exclusive messages in a sequencer. Some system exclusive messages involve two way commu-nications, and a sequencer is unlikely to be able to handle this properly. Some sequencers are simply not designed to be able to deal with any system exclusive messages, and will simply filter them out. In general, facilities to generate and deal with system exclusive messages are improving, but they may never be as straightforward to deal with as program change messages for this type of control.

A further point in favour of using program change messages for general control purposes is that they are recognised by many items of equipment, and one message can be used to set several items of equipment to the desired state. You can use one program change message at the beginning of a sequence to set up several items of equipment with the correct sound data loaded, the right audio mixer settings, the right MIDI patch, the correct digital effect selected, etc. These are channel messages though, and if there are several devices operating on different channels, they will each require a separate program change message on the appropriate channel.

Further program change messages can be used to alter the settings of any device during the course of a piece. There is a slight problem here in that you might wish to alter only one or two items in the system, but have everything on one channel. Perhaps more realistically, you might have a number of channels in use, but with some devices sharing channels. There is no really easy way around this problem since MIDI devices can not usually be set to selectively ignore certain program change messages. Any built-in filtering that can be applied to program change messages will usually only permit all program messages to be accepted, or all of them to be ignored.

The usual solution to the problem is to have the same set of parameters available under different program numbers, as and where necessary. This is not usually too difficult to set up, as many MIDI devices permit sets of data to be copied from one program number to another. With this method, although (say) a synthesizer may be altered from program number 5 to program number 6, by having the same parameters for both these programs there will be no change in the sound from the instrument. Although it will have obeyed the message, its sound will not alter, and it will appear to have ignored it. Other devices in the system could have different sets of data for programs 5 and 6, and would produce a noticeable change when the message was issued. This method of using program change messages needs some careful planning and setting up, but it gives tremendous versatility, and it is usually well worth making the effort.

Keyed-up

It is perhaps worth mentioning that some MIDI devices now have the ability to use note on and note off messages to control some of their functions. I suppose that strictly speaking this type of thing falls outside the MIDI specification, which really allows only for note on and note off messages to control notes in instruments. Although this method of control perhaps goes slightly against the spirit of MIDI, and its fairly strict standards, it is in many ways a very elegant way of handling things.

In order to generate suitable control signals for a device that can use this method of control you need nothing more than a MIDI keyboard, or a MIDI keyboard instrument. In other words, something that is probably present in every MIDI system. Each note can toggle a different function on and off, enabling a large number of functions to be controlled if desired (and if you can remember what each key does). This system is not restricted to simple switching of this type, and each note can be used to select a different set of parameters. In effect, note on and note off messages are then acting as program change messages. Obviously any sequencer can handle simple note on and note off messages properly, and this system could also provide a convenient method of control for "live" performances.

Final points

Designing a method of connection for a MIDI system is really not very difficult provided if you understand the basic principles of chain systems, merging, etc. Of equal importance, you must be clear in your mind about how the system will be used. If you are vague about this, you can not set about logically working out the correct interconnections. With all design work you should accurately define the problem first, and solve it second. What devices will act as controllers, and what will they need to control? Having worked this out, you can then set about finding a way of getting the output of each controller connected through to the appropriate slave devices.

Where two controllers will operate the same slave devices, at the very least a MIDI switcher will be required. Frequently reconnecting and rearranging leads is not a good idea. MIDI sockets are usually tucked away at the rear of equipment where they are difficult to get at, and continual plugging and unplugging will probably damage the connectors and leads before too long. If you will need to reconfigure the system more than occasionally, invest in the proper switching equipment. Of course, if you need to use two controllers simultaneously, a proper merge unit must be used to combine their output signals into a coherent stream of messages. With a very large system that will need frequent reconfiguring, a MIDI patchbay is likely to be well worth the cost.

Once you have decided how everything is to be connected together, sketch out the system showing every connection, and work out carefully where the signal from each controller will go. If there are any switch-over units in the system, work out the signal routes for every combination of switch settings that you will use. When working out a system in your mind it is very easy to overlook something, but if you put things down on paper and check everything through, any silly mistakes should soon be spotted.

The classic mistakes are a break in the "chain" somewhere along the line so that part of the system is isolated, or a complete loop, causing the controller to be fed with its own input signal. You need to be especially careful when using merge units or the THRU facility of a sequencer, as a loop can then cause data to circulate around the system indefinitely, causing the system to crash. Remember that OUT and THRU sockets are different, and that you can only take both the output signal of a unit, and the signal fed to its input, with the aid of a MIDI merge unit or some form of built-in THRU facility.

If you set about things logically and sensibly, you should soon devise a setup that suits your requirements. Be prepared to experiment a little. You may overlook something when designing the system, but with a little thought and experimentation you should soon get things sorted out. MIDI outputs have current limiting to protect then in the event of errors, and there is no real risk to the hardware in experimenting with various setups. If you get it wrong the system will not function properly, but the equipment should suffer no ill effects whatever.

3

MIDI troubleshooting

If you use a MIDI system for any length of time you are almost certain to encounter a problem with things not behaving in the expected manner. This may be in the form of an instrument or even several units in the system operating in an erratic and unreliable fashion. More usually, the problem is one of an instrument failing to do anything at all. There are a number of possible causes for problems with MIDI systems, but these basically boil down to the following general categories:

> Faulty equipment
> Broken MIDI lead
> One of the units not set up correctly

If you go about things in the right way, it is usually not too difficult to track down the cause of the problem, and with luck it can be easily rectified. If the problem is due to a faulty item of equipment I would certainly not recommend that you try do-it-yourself repairs. Modern electronic music equipment is extremely complex and uses many components that are easily damaged. In many cases you would not be able to get suitable spare parts anyway, as MIDI equipment tends to contain a lot of custom made components for which there is no readily available "off the shelf" alternative. Even if you could get suitable replacement parts, fitting them is often a fairly skilled job. Any slight carelessness could easily result in further damage and more spare parts being required! Repairing MIDI equipment is an aspect of MIDI troubleshooting that we will certainly not pursue further here.

Cables

Probably the least reliable aspect of most MIDI systems is the connecting leads. If a system is wired up and then the leads are left completely undisturbed thereafter, the leads should easily outlast everything else in the system. In reality, this does not often happen. Leads tend to dangle on the floor where they get kicked around, and systems are reconfigured from time to time. This can result in the connections inside the plug coming adrift. Leads are also vulnerable at the points where they enter the plugs. There tends to be a lot of flexing of the cable at these points, which in the medium to long term quite often results in a break in the cable.

If you have some form of continuity tester, which for this type of testing needs to be nothing more elaborate than a simple torch bulb and battery type, you can test a MIDI lead by checking for a connection between each pin of one plug and the corresponding pins of the other plug. There are no crossed leads in a MIDI cable. Pin 2 on one plug connects to pin 2 on the other plug, pin 4 connects to pin 4, and pin 5 connects to pin 5, as shown in Figure 3.1. If you are handy with a soldering iron there is no difficulty in making up your own MIDI lead from a couple of 5 way (180 degree) DIN plugs and a length of twin screened cable.

Pins 1 and 3 of both plugs are left unconnected incidentally. If a continuity test should indicate that these pins are connected together it does not matter, since these pins are not connected to anything on the sockets of MIDI equipment. Consequently, any connections between these pins in the lead will be irrelevant, and they can not stop the sys-

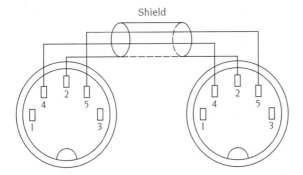

Figure 3.1 The interconnections in a MIDI lead. Check also for short circuits between adjacent pins of each connector.

tem from working properly. In some ready-made MIDI leads these pins do seem to be connected, which would suggest that they were originally intended for audio use rather than to provide interconnections in a MIDI system. Unless you are trying to use cables that are something approaching the maximum permissible length of 15 metres, and audio cable is quite good enough for the digital signals of MIDI (which are not at a particularly high frequency).

Testing, testing

An alternative method of testing a MIDI cable, and what is probably a better one, is to first connect two MIDI units together with a cable that is known to be functioning properly. Then establish contact between the two units via the MIDI link, and check that everything is working correctly. Next replace the good lead with the suspect one. If this does not provide a link between the two MIDI units, then the cable is faulty. When a cable becomes faulty it often provides an intermittent contact, which in a MIDI context means that at times things may seem to be functioning perfectly, while at others part of the system will go "dead". Rather than no connection through the cable at all, there might be an unreliable contact which results in any units fed via that cable operating in an erratic fashion. For example, some notes may be missed out, or (more obviously) some may be left playing indefinitely. A faulty cable can usually be coaxed into failing by simply shaking the lead around a little, or pulling on it gently. Breaks in cables are usually close to one or other of the plugs, so try flexing the leads at both these points. It is always a good idea to try some gentle pulling and flexing if a suspect lead seems to be performing satisfactorily when tested.

Locating a suspect lead, even in a complex system, should not be difficult. With a star system, if one unit goes "dead" it is likely that the lead which connects that unit to the THRU box is faulty. It could be that the MIDI unit itself has gone faulty, but unless you have reason to believe that this is the case, such as the normal start-up display failing to appear, it would probably be best to check the cable first. If nothing works in a star system, then it is probably the cable from the controller to the THRU box that is the cause of the problem. Again, you can not rule out the possibility that one of the pieces of hardware is faulty (such as the controller or the THRU box in this case), but unless there is some reason to believe that an item of hardware is malfunctioning, it is probably best to check the cable first.

With the chain method of connection a faulty cable will not only cut off the signal to the item of equipment it feeds into, but it will also cut off the signal to any subsequent units in the chain. The faulty cable in a chain system is therefore the one ahead of the first unit in the system which is not receiving a signal. As with the star system, you can not be sure that the problem is due to a faulty cable. There is the possibility that a fault in one of the pieces of hardware is resulting in the signal failing to get from the IN socket to the THRU one. As before, unless you have reason to suspect that an item of equipment is faulty, it is best to check the cable first.

If a cable is found to be faulty and it uses plugs of a type that can be opened up, it is worth doing so and inspecting the connections. If a lead has pulled away from its pin of the plug, it is not too difficult to solder it back in place. DIN plugs are notoriously fiddly to deal with though, and you will need a steady hand to do this. It is a job that is much easier if you fix the plug in a small vice. If the connections are all intact, then the problem must be due to a break in the cable. The break is likely to be close to one of the plugs. Therefore, if you trim about 100 to 150 millimetres of cable from the end of each lead and then reconnect the plugs, with a little luck this will give you a serviceable cable that is still of adequate length. If this does not do the trick, then it is probably best to fit a new piece of cable, or to simply buy a new MIDI lead.

Many ready-made MIDI cables now use moulded plugs, which can not be opened up so that the connections can be checked and repaired if necessary. If one of these should become faulty it is probably best just to throw it away and buy a new one.

Signal checking

If the cables are all present and correct, either one of the units in the system is faulty, or it is not set up correctly. The complexity of modern electronic musical instruments, plus what are often considerably less than straightforward methods of controlling the various parameters, make it relatively easy to get an instrument in the wrong MIDI mode, set to the wrong channel, or even to have the MIDI input deactivated. It is worth carefully checking that a MIDI unit is properly set up before deciding to take it back to the shop for repair. The obvious exception is where a unit shows clear signs of being faulty. If the display fails to operate, or if it switches on but just shows random characters, if there seems to be something drastically wrong with the audio output quality, or anything of this general type, it is unlikely that a MIDI fault or the unit being incorrectly set up has anything to do with the problem.

The first step when checking for something in the system that is not set up correctly is to ensure that the controller is sending out the right messages. In order to do this you need some form of MIDI analyser. This can be a piece of hardware designed especially for MIDI troubleshooting, a computer running suitable software, or you may be able to improvise using a MIDI instrument. If we consider MIDI analyser units first, these vary somewhat in complexity. For most checking one of the more simple units will suffice, and these generally have a number of light emitting diodes to indicate message types and channels. A typical front panel for a device of this type would look something along the lines of Figure 3.2. If a note off message on channel 3 should be received, for example, both the note off and channel 3 l.e.d.s would briefly flash on. If a clock message is received, the system message l.e.d. flashes briefly, as does the clock l.e.d.

A simple analyser of this type does not give any indication of data byte values. This precludes its use for checking that a velocity sensitive keyboard is functioning correctly, ascertaining that the right note values are being produced, and this sort of thing. This is not of great importance for the type of testing we are concerned with here. The main requirements are to be able to check that channel messages are on the right channel or channels, and that note on, note off, and possibly other types of message are actually being generated.

More sophisticated analysers have been produced, and these operate in a variety of ways. A typical arrangement would have a two digit seven segment display to show the received bytes in hexadecimal form, or perhaps eight l.e.d.s to show the binary pattern. There could be something more sophisticated, such as an alpha-numeric display which would show messages such as "DATA 64", or "NOTE ON", so that it would be unnecessary for the user to recognise or look up the displayed code numbers. A memory circuit would be used to store (say) the first 1024 bytes received after the "start" button was operated. The user could then use the display to show any desired byte stored in

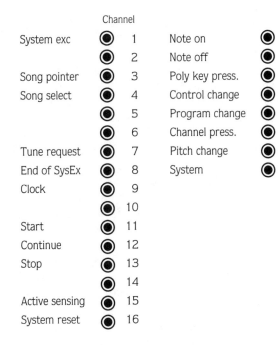

Figure 3.2 The simpler MIDI analysers have a simple display of this type to show the messages received and the channels in use.

memory. In this way you can work through the received data, checking the message types, channel numbers, note values, etc.

A unit of this kind is obviously suitable for the type of checking involved when troubleshooting on a MIDI system, but it is really somewhat over specified. Devices of this type are really intended for checking that each function of a MIDI controller is operating correctly, and are only likely to be fully exploited by someone who undertakes servicing of MIDI equipment. For present purposes, a simple MIDI analyser will probably tell you all that you need to know. On the other hand, I suppose that with the aid of a comprehensive analyser you can thoroughly check out the controller, leaving absolutely no doubt as to whether or not it is functioning correctly.

Computer analyser

A computer having a MIDI interface can act as a first class MIDI analyser. You do not even need to run a sophisticated analyser program, and just a few lines of BASIC will often suffice. Assuming for the moment that you wish to use a ready-made program of reasonable sophistication, the availability of this type of software depends very much on the particular computer you use. There should be little difficulty in finding a suitable program for a computer such as one in the Atari ST series, which are very popular with MIDI users. There will probably be at least one public domain or shareware program that will fit the bill and cost little or nothing. With a machine that is not much used by MIDI enthusiasts there is little chance of finding any suitable ready-made software. In the computing world life is generally much easier if you stay in the mainstream rather than opting for rare and unusual software and hardware.

A computer based MIDI analyser usually provides facilities that are similar to ordinary analysers of the type just described. The screen display would typically have a number of labelled boxes for channel numbers, plus further boxes for the various message types. A box flashes to a different colour, or into inverse video, when an appropriate message is received. Computer based analysers often have a facility that enables received MIDI data to be stored in memory and then inspected in detail. Some have what I suppose could be termed a "slow motion action replay" facility. In other words, you record a rapid sequence of MIDI messages into the unit, and then have the unit analyse the recorded messages in slow motion so that you can see exactly what is happening. The power of modern microcomputers is such that a computer based analyser can have virtually any feature the programmer sees fit to include.

DIY analyser

If you have a computer with a MIDI interface it will probably not be too difficult to write a program that will make it act as a simple analyser. MIDI signals tend to be groups of bytes send in rapid succession, and this can slightly complicate matters. You need to have a fairly fast programming language in order to keep up with the bursts of MIDI activity with 100% reliability. Alternatively, the MIDI interface should be one that is properly supported by firmware and (or) the programming language so that received bytes are stored in a buffer until they are read. This aspect of things will not be covered in more detail here, since it is fully discussed in the chapter on MIDI programming.

Assuming that you have a computer with a MIDI interface, and a programming language that can be used to read the MIDI port reliably, a MIDI analyser can be produced using a program that simply prints on the screen any values received via the MIDI port. This program for the Atari ST computers, which is written in Fast BASIC, shows how simple a MIDI analyser can be.

```
REPEAT UNTIL
PRINT (INP(3) AND 255)
UNTIL FALSE
```

This simply loops indefinitely, reading the MIDI port each time a fresh byte of data is available. The returned values are sixteen bit types, of which the eight least significant bits are the valid MIDI values. The "AND 255" part of the second line is used to remove the unwanted upper eight bits. No equivalent of this is needed when reading most MIDI ports.

Printing to the screen is a relatively slow business with most computers, and in some cases it would be better to store values read from the port in memory until a certain number had been received, and to then print them on the screen. This would prevent the time taken to write values to the screen causing a malfunction. With the ST computers there is proper support for the built-in MIDI port, with values being read from the port and stored in a buffer until they are read by a programming language via the appropriate system calls. Provided MIDI messages are not received at a very high rate, the buffer will not become overloaded and reliable results will be obtained. In practice there should be no difficulty in keeping the rate at which data is fed to the unit down to a reasonable level. It is advisable to do this anyway, so that the screen is not continuously scrolling, making it difficult to read the displayed values.

Although this type of analyser is very simple, it is very revealing. You can check that two suitable sets of three values are produced each time a key is pressed and released. You will see whether the note off instructions are standard note off types, or note on messages having a velocity value of 0. Channel numbers can be checked, as can note values. If the keyboard is a touch sensitive type, you can check that the velocity values respond properly to the force with which keys are played. If the keyboard is one which has only about six velocity levels, this will become apparent, with the same few velocity values being produced time and time again. In fact it is possible to thoroughly investigate virtually every aspect of a MIDI controller using a simple analyser of this type.

Obviously refinements can be added, with the computer being used to decode messages and display them along these lines

```
Note on - Channel 3
Note 65
Velocity 64
```

However, the added convenience might not be worth the substantial amount of time it would probably take to write a program of this type. There is a simple refinement to the program that will make it much easier to use, and this is to have it split header bytes into two nibbles. This makes it much easier to work out the message type, and the channel number where appropriate. This simple Fast BASIC program for the Atari STs provides this splitting of header bytes.

```
REPEAT
X = (INP(3) AND 255)
IF (X > 127) THEN PROCSPLIT ELSE PRINT X
UNTIL FALSE
DEF PROCSPLIT
Y = X AND 240
Z = X AND 15
PRINT Y,Z
ENDPROC
```

The program reads in values from the MIDI port, and then tests to see if they are higher than 127 in value (which they will only be if they are status bytes). If not, then they are printed to screen. If a status byte is detected, the program branches to the procedure (a form of sub-program or subroutine) called "PROCSPLIT". This uses bitwise ANDing (a process explained in the chapter on MIDI programming) to put the most and least significant nibbles into variables "Y" and "Z".

These values are then printed side-by-side on the screen. You soon learn to recognise the common header byte values (144 for note, 128 for note off, etc.), and interpreting the displayed data is usually quite easy. The tables provided at the end of Chapter 1 should soon help to sort things out if you get into difficulties when trying to interpret results.

Many computer based sequencer programs have some MIDI analyser capabilities. They often permit the sequences stored in memory to be examined in minute detail, with message types, note values, velocity values, etc., all being shown. Some even have some form of real-time display of received message types etc. You need to be a little cautious when using a sequencer for analyser purposes though. If erroneous messages are received, they may simply be ignored, rather than producing some form of error message display. In many ways a simple display of received values is best for detailed checking of MIDI data streams. It leaves little scope for errors to slip through unnoticed.

Improvisation

Given that a MIDI analyser is something that might be needed only occasionally, the cost of a unit of this type, even one of the more simple ones, is probably too high for many MIDI users to deem it worthwhile buying one. A computer type, provided you already have a suitable computer (as many MIDI users do), is a more attractive proposition. A public domain analyser program will cost no more than a few pounds, or a simple routine of your own will cost nothing. The problem with a computer based system is that the computer is likely to be the controller in your MIDI system. If the computer can multi-task, it might be possible to run a sequencer program while at the same time monitoring the output from that program using the analyser program. The MIDI input and output sockets of the computer (or its add-on MIDI interface) would have to be linked in order to facilitate this monitoring. In practice there are still relatively few computers that can reliably undertake true multi-tasking. Even if you do have one of those that can, it might not have enough memory to run a complex sequencer program and an analyser type.

Of course, this problem is not insurmountable, and there is almost certain to be some other MIDI control device (such as a keyboard instrument) which can be temporarily used as the controller for the system while trying to locate the fault. If necessary, the output of this instrument can be checked using the computer based MIDI analyser. It could be that the setup you are using when the problem arises does not have the computer as the controller anyway, so that there is no conflict if it is used to run the MIDI analyser program. If you have upgraded from an old 8 bit computer to a 16 bit type, and have kept the 8 bit system, do not overlook the possibility of using the old computer as a MIDI analyser.

An alternative to using any form of analyser is to utilise another instrument to check the output of the controller. It is a good idea to have in any MIDI system a keyboard instrument that is easily set to mode 3, and to receive on a particular MIDI channel. It is also helpful if the instrument can have its keyboard switched to send on any desired MIDI channel, so that it can also be used to provide a test signal if necessary. I find that my Casio CZ1 is ideal when checking new pieces of equipment, new configurations, etc., but no doubt there are many other keyboard instruments which are equally good for this type of thing.

Some instruments can use their display to give a crude MIDI analyser action, and obviously a unit of this type is also well suited to MIDI testing. Most instruments have nothing more than an indicator light which flashes when a MIDI signal is received, and some even lack this. Do not be misled by MIDI input signal l.e.d.s which fail to operate, suggesting that the unit is not receiving a MIDI signal at all. It seems to be normal for these l.e.d.s to flash on only when a MIDI message that is relevant to the unit is received. If the messages are not on a channel where the unit is active, the l.e.d. will not light up. An instrument which provides no help beyond a MIDI input indicator can still act as a useful MIDI testing device provided it is simple and direct to use, so that you can be sure it is operating on the right channel, in the right mode, etc.

When using an instrument as an analyser it is basically just a matter of switching it to mode 3, the right channel, and then monitoring its audio output to see if it responds to the received messages in the right way. If the unit fails to do anything, it is likely that the messages are not being sent on the expected channel. Switch the instrument through the MIDI channels until it responds to the controller, and you will then know what channel the messages are being transmitted on. This will not in itself tell you what is wrong with the setting up of the controller, but it will provide a good clue. Once you know what channel the messages are actually on it may well be fairly obvious where you have gone wrong.

It may be apparent, regardless of what type of MIDI monitoring setup is used, that the controller is providing an output that is erroneous in some way. This can manifest itself in a number of ways, from something relatively mild, such as a certain type of message always being missing or the same note value always being used, through to things such as only the odd byte being sent here and there, or the bytes all being just random values.

This general type of thing, whether the corruption of the data is mild or severe, is usually indicative of a serious fault in the controller hardware. If the problem is in a computer based sequencer, it could be that the disk from which the program is loaded has become corrupted, causing a fault in the running of the program. This is unlikely, as even very minor corruption of computer programs usually results in them crashing totally out of controlling or simply coming to an abrupt halt as soon as the faulty code is run. However, it might be worthwhile making a fresh copy of the program from the master disk or disks, and running it again.

When using any equipment that contains a microprocessor it is as well to bear in mind that noise spikes on the mains supply, lightning, static discharges, or other electrical noise can cause the unit to malfunction. Again, this will usually result in the unit coming to an abrupt halt, or crashing totally out of control. However, it can sometimes result in the unit functioning to some degree, but in an erratic fashion with numerous errors. Static discharges can cause damage to microprocessors or other sensitive electronic components, but in most cases normal operation can be restored simply by switching the unit off, waiting a few seconds, and then switching it on again. Remember that computers are not the only pieces of equipment that contain microprocessors. Virtually every piece of MIDI gear contains at least one microprocessor, and is therefore vulnerable to this problem.

Faulty setup

If the leads are all right, and the MIDI controller is sending the right data, then either the receiving device is faulty or not set up correctly. Modern MIDI instruments are noted for, in the main, being considerably less than straightforward to set up ready for use. There are often dozens, or even hundreds of functions accessed via a few push button switches, with the only help coming from what is often a small display showing rather cryptic messages. The controls of some MIDI units bear an ominous resemblance to an electronic combination lock! Mistakes are easily made, especially when you are dealing with a unit for the first few times. If the unit is obviously completely "dead", or faulty in some other way, then it should obviously be returned for servicing. If the display is operative, and the control buttons produce changes on the display, but control via MIDI is not as expected, there is a reasonable chance that the unit is functioning, but is not set up correctly.

The only way to check this possibility is to carefully read through the instruction manual and once again go through the various processes needed to set up the unit in the desired fashion. There are certain aspects which are worthy of special attention. Does the unit have some form of MIDI on/off control? Some instruments have a MIDI on/off button which can easily be knocked and accidentally toggled to the off state. Sometimes a series of key presses are needed in order to deactivate MIDI, but you might have hit this combination by mistake while trying to adjust some other facet of MIDI.

Is the unit simply operating on the wrong channel? Try driving it from a keyboard or other controller that can be easily switched through the full range of MIDI channels, so that you can check to see if it is responding to any channel or channels. A do-it-yourself computer program to output a few note on and note off messages on channels 1 to 16, in sequence, can be handy for checking purposes. Try setting the unit to omni on, so that it should respond to messages on any channel. This might enable you to re-establish MIDI contact with the device, so that you can have a second attempt at getting it set up correctly.

If the unit is responding to some types of message, but not to others, check the MIDI implementation chart to ensure that it supports the features you are trying to use. This may seem like a silly suggestion, but there are a lot of MIDI instruments that have quite full implementations, but still have one or two surprising omissions. With MIDI implementations it is always advisable to take nothing for granted, and to always check just what an instrument can and can not do.

Remember that many MIDI devices have built-in filtering, and can be made to ignore certain types of message. In the case of controllers, they often have some features deactivated, effectively giving filtering of pitch wheel changes etc. on their output signal. It might seem reasonable to assume that everything will function properly unless you specifically deactivate something, but the default settings sometimes have one or two message types in the deactivated state. Do not over-look the possibility that you might have accidentally switched off a MIDI function by accident, or the unit might have glitched and erroneously switched it off. Go through the appropriate set of control sequences to reactivate the "dead" feature, to see if this clears the problem.

Replace back-up batteries

A fair proportion of modern electronic instruments have back-up batteries for their memory circuits. These batteries are mostly designed to last a very long time indeed. About five years is the normal lifespan. Usually the idea is to change the battery just within what I sup-pose could be termed its "expiry date", so that the data in the memory circuits is preserved. The supply is normally maintained by a high value capacitor during the changeover.

Probably few people remember to do this, and I think that it is quite likely that many people trade-in instruments before the first bat-tery change is needed. The implication for someone who has bought a secondhand instrument which is a few years old, is that its battery is likely to fail before too long. Prevention is better than cure, and if in doubt it is probably best to fit a new battery (or to have a new one fit-ted if it is a non-user changeable type). Apart from the inconvenience of having an instrument "die" on you, putting back all the lost data can take a lot of time and effort.

4
MIDI gadgets

Probably when you think of MIDI equipment, it is major pieces of gear such as computers, synthesisers, audio mixers, and sound samplers that spring to mind. In truth, it is likely that the vast majority of MIDI equipment is of this type, but there are also many more minor MIDI units available. These are devices that will make up for a shortcoming in a major piece of equipment, add some useful and novel facility to a MIDI system, or in some way enhance a MIDI system. They are normally of no worth as self contained devices used in isolation. In this chapter we will consider some typical MIDI add-ons, and the ways in which they can be used.

MIDI hardware in general seems to change at a fairly rapid rate, but the add-on devices seem to undergo changes at a rate which is even more rapid than the MIDI average. Apart from changes to existing MIDI gadgets, the rate at which devices disappear from the market and new ones appear is quite high. Consequently, in this chapter it is only possible to talk in general terms about the types of MIDI add-on that are available. If you are thinking about buying a MIDI gadget it will be necessary to study the advertisements in electronic music magazines in order to ascertain exactly what devices are available at the time, and what they can do. There may be something that suits your requirements, or you might be out of luck. Note that in this chapter we will not bother with any devices concerned with the routing of MIDI signals, synchronisation, or MIDI troubleshooting, as these are dealt with at some length in separate chapters.

Step on it

One general category of MIDI add-on is the MIDI pedal. In the past MIDI has tended to be the province of those who are interested in sequencing applications using what are often large systems, or small systems that eventually grow into quite large ones. MIDI rapidly gained a dominant role in many music studios, both of the home and professional varieties. It has tended to be used much less for live performances. MIDI pedals are mainly intended to make MIDI more usable in live performance, although they can be used to good effect in a studio setup as well.

These units provide a variety of functions. At a most basic level there is the "all notes off" pedal, which simply sends a MIDI all notes off message when it is activated. An alternative method is to have the unit send a note off message for every note on every channel. This might seem to be doing things the hard way, but it is more reliable because not all instruments recognise an all notes off message. Presumably the idea is that this unit's output signal should be merged with that of the MIDI controller, so that in the event of a fault it can be used to send a message that will switch off any droning notes.

This method would appear to be something less than 100% reliable in that if the problem should be due to a damaged cable or disconnected lead, the all notes off message would not get through to any equipment that had suffered from *MIDI interruptus*. Of course, the pedal could be used to turn off any droning notes after the cable had been restored to normality. Active sensing would seem to offer a better solution to problems with damaged cables etc., but as yet only a fairly small proportion of instruments seem to support this feature.

Another form of MIDI pedal is one that can send MIDI controller messages. The basic idea of these units is to provide pedal control of some function of an instrument in the system. In fact a unit of this type can be used with just as gainfully with a single instrument as with a complex MIDI system. Most instruments enable at least a few basic functions to be controlled via MIDI control messages, and units of this type can normally be used to operate as soft or sustain pedals, an alternative to the modulation wheel, etc. Some units have multiple pedals so that they can be used to control several functions.

In a similar vein, some pedals provide pitch wheel change messages. These obviously provide a foot operated alternative to the instrument's pitch wheel.

Some MIDI pedal units are now quite sophisticated, offering perhaps as many as four pedals which each one programmable and able to control more than a single function. At a most basic level, this multiple control facility could be used to permit control of the master volume control setting, but on several channels. Remember that MIDI control messages are channel types, and in a system that has several instruments (or virtual instruments) on different channels, a single control message will control only one instrument. In order to control every instrument in unison it might be necessary to have each control change message sent on all sixteen MIDI channels. At least one MIDI pedal unit is capable of doing this. You are not even restricted to controlling the same parameter on each channel. If you should wish to operate control number 7 on two channels in unison with control 4 on another three channels, this is easily achieved. You can even control several controls at once on the same channel (e.g. a pedal could vary controls 4, 7, and 23 on channel 5).

Programmable pedals are usually capable of sending more than just control change messages, or control change and pitch wheel types. You can specify a string of values to be sent each time the pedal is activated, and can also specify which byte or bytes should contain data read from the pedal's position. In this way it is possible to control virtually any MIDI function, or several functions simultaneously. You are not restricted to channel messages, and can use the pedal to produce system types if desired. It would presumably even be possible to implement system exclusive messages, provided they are types that do not involve a two way exchange of information, or the sending of very long strings of bytes. Bearing in mind that some devices give better access to the control circuits via system exclusive messages than they do by way of MIDI control messages, the ability to use system exclusive messages could be crucial if a sophisticated pedal unit is to be exploited to the full.

Although any type of MIDI message can be generated, I suppose that not all types could be put to good use with a pedal unit. With a bit of imagination it should be quite easy to put a unit of this type to good use though, especially for live performances. One kind of message which could be appropriate with a unit of this type is the aftertouch type. In this context the channel variety would be used, as the pedal would then control the volume etc. of any note on the channel in question.

Due process

A large percentage of MIDI add-ons are concerned with taking in a MIDI signal, processing it in some way, and then sending on the doctored signal to all or part of the system. Just how many units in the system receive the altered signal depends on the method of connection used, and exactly where in the system the processor is inserted. Finding the right method of connection and insertion point for a MIDI processor can often be crucial in obtaining precisely the desired result.

There must be almost endless ways in which a MIDI signal can be processed in order to give some enhancement or other. At a very basic level there are the units which are sometimes called channelisers. All a unit of this type does is to alter the status bytes of channel messages so that they are switched to a different channel. However, this process is usually applied in some highly selective manner in order to obtain precisely the desired effect. A common use for a channeliser is with an old MIDI instrument that only provides operation on channel 1. Suppose that the instrument can only transmit on channel 1, but that for some reason you need to send messages on channel 3. The output of the keyboard would be sent through the channeliser, which would detect channel message header bytes, and change the channel nibble from 0000 to 0010 (the channel 1 and channel 3 binary values respectively).

The channeliser might be capable of doing something more clever than this basic channel swapping. This would normally take the form of providing a keyboard split. In other words, it would provide the keyboard splitting function that is built into some instruments, and which has half the keyboard operating on one MIDI channel, and the other half operating on a different MIDI channel. In fact the split point might be user selectable, rather than just being preset at the half way point. Also, it might be possible to have a three way split, and operation on three MIDI channels. Providing this facility using an external channeliser requires a more sophisticated unit than one that provides simple channel switching. The unit must read in the status byte and then the first data byte. The status byte is then altered, or not, depending on the note value in the first data byte.

There is a potential problem with this type of processing in that the unit might be called upon to handle more than just note on and note off channel messages. In the case of polyphonic key pressure messages, which contain note values, the unit can process the messages in exactly the same way as note on/off types. However, other channel messages do not contain note values, and the channeliser has no way of knowing which channel or channels they should be directed to. This basically boils down to leaving these other messages untouched, switching them to a user specified channel, or generating additional messages so that any message of this type received at the input is sent on all the channels in use from the output. The last method is probably the best one, but is the one that is least likely to be available. It has a potential flaw in that the additional messages generated could produce MIDI choke at times.

A channeliser can also be used at the input of a MIDI device. Again, suppose you have a couple of instruments that will only respond to messages sent on channel 1. On the face of it there is no way that these can be sequenced independently. With the aid of a channeliser this is possible though. The system illustrated in Figure 4.1 shows how

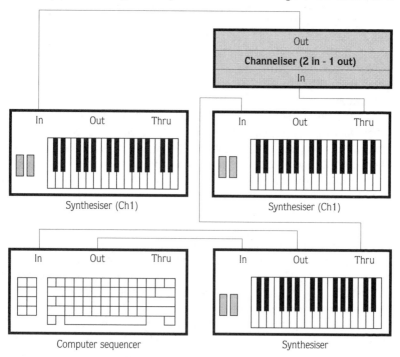

Figure 4.1 Using a channeliser to permit independent sequencing of two channel 1 instruments.

this is achieved. This is a system which utilises the chain method of connection. The two channel 1 instruments are at the end of the chain, but have the channeliser connected between them. The channeliser is used to switch channel 2 messages onto channel 1.

The first of these instruments responds to channel 1 messages, but ignores channel 2 messages. The channeliser switches these channel 2 messages onto channel 1, and the second instrument then responds to them. With a very simple channeliser this will not provide quite the desired effect, since channel 1 messages would be fed through to the second of the instruments, which would then respond to them. The second instrument would therefore respond to both channel 1 and channel 2 messages. It can be made to respond to channel 2 alone if the channeliser is sophisticated enough to filter out channel 1

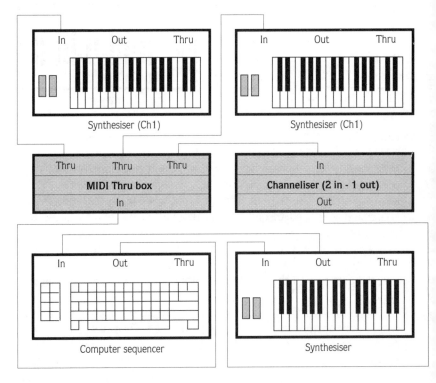

Figure 4.2 A system similar to the one of Figure 4.1, but using the star system.

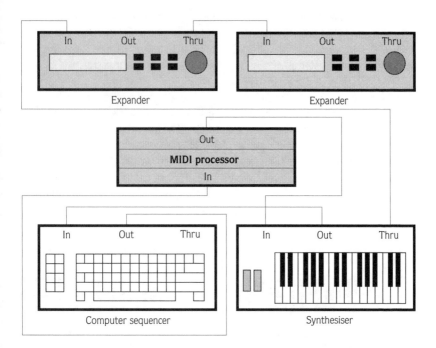

Figure 4.3 The method of processing the signal to the whole system when using the chain system of connection.

messages, or to simply switch them onto another channel so that they are ignored by the second instrument.

It should be apparent from this that when using MIDI processing equipment you need to give careful thought to the exact process the unit is providing. Things are often nothing like as straightforward as they at first appear. A processor might give the desired effect, but it might also have unwanted and unacceptable side effects. You also need to give careful thought to the positioning of the processor in the system.

In the example of Figure 4.1 it is obviously crucial that the processor only doctors the signal received by the second of the two channel 1 instruments. In the example setup the chain method of connection is used, but the same effect could be achieved with the star method of connection, as shown in Figure 4.2. If a processor must process the signal fed to the whole system, then it must be connected at the output of the controller. This is easily achieved using the chain

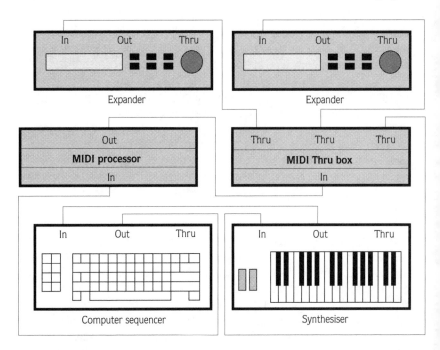

Figure 4.4 Using the star system to process the signal to the entire system.

method of connection (Figure 4.3), but is less easy with the star method. Even if the controller has multiple outputs, it will still be necessary to use a THRU box, as shown in Figure 4.4.

Perfect harmony

Another form of processor is the MIDI harmoniser. An ordinary harmoniser processes the audio output of an instrument. It generates tones that will harmonise with the input note, and mixes them with the input signal. For example, the harmoniser could generate a note a fifth higher than the input signal, giving a richer and more "fat" sound. Audio harmonisers tend to be less than perfect, as it can be difficult to quickly determine the pitch of the input signal and produce a signal that is offset by the correct interval. Even with simple input waveforms such as sinewave and squarewave, there can be problems in getting a unit of this type to work really well. The output waveforms from musical instruments are often very complex, possibly with a strong harmonic content that makes the true frequency of the signal difficult to determine. Due to the difficulties associated with even simple monophonic operation, most audio harmonisers make no attempt at polyphonic operation.

Matters are much easier with a MIDI harmoniser as it operates on the MIDI signal, generating additional note on and note off messages to produce the harmonising notes. There is obviously no difficulty in determining the pitch of notes from the MIDI messages, or in generating additional messages having the appropriate offset in the pitch data byte. It is perfectly possible to have each note generate several new notes if desired. There is no need to have fixed offsets, and an "intelligent" unit with a microprocessor controller can generate quite complex harmonies.

Any note messages received will result in the appropriate additional note messages being generated, no matter how many notes are received. This gives polyphonic operation with as many notes playing at a time as you desire. However, with any unit that has more messages at the output than are received at the input it is as well to bear in mind that there is a risk of choke occurring at times of high activity. Also, remember that it is no good having a unit that generates complex harmonies unless you have instruments with enough voices to actually play all the notes. Unlike an audio harmoniser, a MIDI type normally just generates extra MIDI note on and note off messages, and has no sound generating circuits of its own.

Transposing

In a similar vein to harmonising, some processors provide transposition. In other words, they shift received notes up or down by a specified musical interval. Unlike MIDI harmonising, transposition does not result in extra notes being generated − it simply modifies those that are received. However, if the unprocessed notes are played on one instrument, and the processed notes are played on a second, the effect is a form of harmonising.

Filtering

A MIDI filter is a device which selectively removes MIDI messages. One reason for doing this is in order to avoid problems with MIDI choke. Unfortunately, it is not just a matter of inserting a MIDI filter at the output of the controller, and removing a few of the less important message types in order to avoid choke problems (see Appendix 1). This will not work at all, since the choke will occur within the controller, causing some messages to be lost. A MIDI filter will simply remove more messages – it will not restore those that have been lost. The only way to properly combat MIDI choke is to ensure that the device generating the MIDI signals never gets an overloaded output in the first place.

With something like a keyboard instrument there is no major risk of MIDI choke occurring. Even if you play as many notes as possible as fast as possible, and get someone to operate the pitch and modulation wheels, the instrument will probably be able to cope. The MIDI output will be sending out an almost constant stream of messages, but these will accurately reflect the playing of the instrument. MIDI choke is most likely to occur when using a sequencer, and building up a multi-track piece. Each track may involve only quite modest amounts of MIDI activity, but with perhaps sixteen or more tracks being played back simultaneously when the finished piece is "performed", at times there could be a massive number of messages to be crammed into a very short period. MIDI choke could then easily occur.

Some sequencers are now quite sophisticated, and if MIDI choke should be unavoidable, they will automatically select the most important messages for transmission while missing out those that are of less importance. Note on and note off messages would have the highest priority, with messages such as pitch bend types having a lower priority. Many sequencers also have the ability to provide filtering of received messages, so that the amount of data per track can be kept down to an acceptable level. Many instruments now seem to have filtering as well, and can be set to ignore certain types of message, or not to transmit certain types. This second feature can obviously be used when laying down tracks, in order to prevent an excessive amount of data per track.

If these filtering facilities are missing from both your sequencer and your instruments, then a MIDI filter unit might be of benefit. However, it is a good idea to check the manuals for the sequencer and instruments very carefully to ensure that you have not overlooked a facility of this type somewhere in the "fine print". It would be very easy to pay out for a MIDI processor that merely duplicated features already available from the equipment, and no doubt a few people do this from time to time! Another point that should not be overlooked is that it is often possible to avoid MIDI choke by simply not using facilities that will generate large amounts of data. Rather than filtering out pitch wheel messages, why not simply leave the pitch wheel untouched? A MIDI instrument normally generates large amounts of data only in response to something you have done – they do not normally generate data of their own volition.

MIDI filtering is not only used as a means of avoiding MIDI choke, and their are a few other uses. These mainly involve having one instrument respond to certain types of message while another one in the system does not. Suppose that in the setup of Figure 4.1 (page 78), the channeliser is replaced by a filter that removes all pitch bend information. The first of the two instruments would respond to pitch bend messages, but the second would not. Once again, this is something that could be achieved without the use of a filter unit if the second instrument had suitable built-in filtering.

Some filters can be set to remove all but system messages, and those messages that are on one particular channel. This gives a sort of channelising, and is useful when used with an instrument that has only omni modes. Normally a unit of this type will respond to messages on any channel, rendering it useless for operation in many multi-instrument sequencing arrangements. Using this type of filter ahead of the unit effectively places it in mode 3 or mode 4 on the channel that the filter does not affect. It can then be used as a normal mode 3 or mode 4 instrument.

Multi-processing

Some MIDI processors are quite complex devices that, instead of being designed to provide one or two specific types of processing, can provide a whole range of processes. As most MIDI processors are based on a microprocessor, giving them the ability to provide a whole range of effects does not greatly boost the amount of hardware required. Most of the extra facilities can be provided solely by additions to the software, and the extra cost involved is largely that of the increased software development. About the only extra hardware needed is a better control panel and display to permit the required facilities to be selected and set up correctly. Some of these multi-processors are actually some other form of MIDI unit to which the processing facilities have been added in order to make the product more attractive to potential purchasers. At least one MIDI patchbay for example, has a wide range of MIDI processes available. Again, the extra hardware needed is minimal, and the extra features are largely provided by additions to the software.

Multi-processors usually provide just about every conceivable type of MIDI processing, including some that are far from being run of the mill. It is probable that these units provide the only off-the-shelf means of obtaining some of the more obscure types of processing. The usual types of processing such as filtering of various types, note transposition, and keyboard splitting should also be present. One of the more rare but potentially very useful types of processing is one which provides a form of channelising. This operates on the basis of having notes left on their existing channel unless the velocity value exceeds a certain value. This might operate in conjunction with a two or three way keyboard split. For example, with a three way split the low, middle, and high notes having low velocity values might be placed on channels 1, 2, and 3 respectively. Those having high velocity values could be placed on channels 4, 5, and 6 respectively.

The keyboard split provides the normal function of permitting different areas of the keyboard to be assigned to totally different sounds. The velocity split could simply be used to provide totally different sounds on loud and soft notes, but it would normally be used to give greater realism when synthesising acoustic instrument sounds. Some instruments sound distinctly different to their normal sounds when played loudly. Probably the most striking examples are the "overblown" woodwind instruments, but most instruments, at the very least, have a noticeably harsher sound when played loudly.

Velocity splits provide a convenient means of switching between two sounds, one representing normal playing and one for loud playing. Some instruments have this type of facility built-in, and where such a facility is available, it is probably best to use it in preference to external processing. A velocity split facility is quite common in sound samplers, but is relatively rare in other types of instrument. Where an instrument does not have this type of facility, an external processor provides a means of obtaining more realistic sounds from the system. Of course, a facility of this type is not restricted to use in simulating acoustic instruments, and it can be used in more imaginative and novel ways if you so desire.

There are many other types of MIDI processing, and it is possible to change any MIDI message to any other type of message. Pitch wheel change messages can be converted to MIDI controller types, so that the pitch wheel can be used to control other functions instead. Processing messages is an aspect of MIDI which is potentially very useful indeed, but it is one which few people seem to have explored. It is something that is well worth investigating.

MIDI to CV

In the pre-MIDI era it was often possible to slave one instrument to another, or to control an instrument using a computer. This was generally only possible with synthesisers, and not even all synthesisers had the necessary sockets. It was quite a common feature though, and even some of the later low cost synthesisers had suitable input and output sockets. There was a slight problem with a lack of true standardisation of synthesiser interfaces, and this often gave problems when using instruments from more than one manufacturer. All analogue synthesisers use the same basic system where notes are switched on and off via one signal, and the pitch is controlled by a second. These are the gate (or trigger) and CV (control voltage) signals.

The gate signal is a digital type which provides an on/off action. It is "high" (logic 1) to represent a depressed key, and "low" (logic 0) to represent all keys in the up position. The control voltage operates on the basis of the higher the note played, the higher the voltage. The most popular control characteristic was the one volt per octave type, but others were used. In fact there was no proper standardisation of either the gate or control voltage signals. This lack of proper standards and the customer dissatisfaction it caused was one of the main motivations for the instrument manufacturers to get together and agree a truly standard digital interface for the next generation of instruments. This standard is, of course, MIDI.

Although the MIDI method of interfacing has practically nothing in common with the old gate/CV method, it is not too difficult to produce converters that will enable MIDI and gate/CV equipped instruments to operate together. There is probably no point in having a unit that converts gate/CV signals into corresponding MIDI types. This would give an extremely crude form of MIDI controller, and would probably not be worth the effort. A conversion in the opposite direction is potentially a more useful one, particularly for someone who already owns one or more analogue synthesisers having gate/CV inputs. This enables the instruments to operate in a MIDI system, although probably only in a limited fashion by modern standards. In many cases such a combination would provide no more than basic pitch control and gating of notes. With suitable hardware a higher degree of control might be available, with the converter unit responding to pitch wheel change messages. Some converters even have CV outputs that reflect the velocity values in received note on messages. With a suitable analogue synthesiser, this signal could be used to control the envelope shaper, or perhaps the v.c.f. (voltage controlled filter), in order to give a form of touch sensitivity.

An obvious problem in using a MIDI to gate/CV converter is that of the potential incompatibility problems that can arise on the output side of the unit. Assuming that no problems of this type arise, or they can be easily solved, a converter could be a useful gadget for someone who has suitable analogue synthesisers, or perhaps for someone who has the opportunity to buy them at low cost. However, as the old analogue synthesisers are rapidly becoming virtual museum pieces, and modern low cost MIDI expanders offer a very high level of performance, using old instruments as part of a modern system is perhaps a less attractive proposition than it once was. Remember that most analogue synthesisers provide only monophonic operation. A modern low cost MIDI rack-mount instrument would typically provide sixteen note polyphony with up to six channels/sounds in use simultaneously. One modern low cost instrument can outperform a whole bank of traditional analogue synthesisers. These days MIDI to CV converters are perhaps of most interest to those who are devoted to the sounds of old analogue instruments, and are determined to have instruments of this type included in their MIDI system regardless of its practicality.

Drum pads

MIDI drum pads probably represent one of the most popular forms of MIDI add-on. Units of this type typically consist of about four to eight drum pads which when struck generate a pair of MIDI note on/note off messages. Usually the note value generated by each pad is programmable, and the velocity value reflects the vigour with which the pad is struck. These are both important factors.

Drum machines, and percussion channels of synthesisers which have this facility, work on the basis of assigning a different sound to each note value. With few exceptions, they do not operate in mode 4 with a different sound assigned to each MIDI channel. Where this option is available, it would often be an inefficient way of doing things anyway. For the drum pads to trigger the desired sounds of the drum machine or synthesiser they must therefore be programmable to provide the right note values. Alternatively, they can provide different but preset note values, with the drum machine or synthesiser (if possible) being set up so that the right sound is activated by each pad.

Obviously the ability to control the dynamics of an instrument is important, as it represents a major way in which feeling can be put into one's playing. With many percussion instruments it is particularly important, as it represents what is often the only way of putting emotion into the playing of the instruments.

Wireless

MIDI provides an operating range of 15 metres, which is adequate for most purposes. There are units which can provide a greater range if necessary. Perhaps of more general appeal, there are devices which avoid the need for connecting cables between the units in a MIDI system. These could be used in a studio, but connecting cables can usually be tidied away out of harm's way in a studio environment without too much difficulty. Units of this type are aimed more at live performances, where there is a greater danger of cables being tripped over. Apart from the danger to life and limb, a kicked cable can have a pretty disastrous affect on the music making. Units of this type can also give greater freedom of movement to those who play instruments (and perform in a manner) that makes this point applicable.

Some of these wireless connecting systems operate using an infra-red link, basically much like that used for many television remote control systems. An alternative approach is to have units that enable MIDI signals to be sent via an ordinary radio microphone link. Radio microphones have, of course, been used by vocalists etc. for a number of years now. Unfortunately, they are unsuitable for use with ordinary MIDI signals. Apart from incompatibility with the current loop system of interfacing used for MIDI, there is a more major problem in that the bandwidth of an audio link is inadequate to handle MIDI signals properly. They become severely "smeared" (like an extremely bad case of so-called MIDI delay), and can not be decoded reliably by the receiving device. Devices that enable MIDI to be sent over normal radio links operate by using compression techniques that permit the signals to be sent via a relatively narrow bandwidth link, and then expanded back into proper MIDI signals again at the receiving end of the system.

Wireless links are no doubt invaluable for those who really need them. Perhaps "wireless" is not a wholly apt term since there can be a fair number of short connecting wires between the units at each end of the system. Despite this, they are still an attractive proposition for someone who does a lot of live performances. Unfortunately, as yet they remain quite expensive, whereas MIDI cables cost just a few pounds.

Wireless systems that enable MIDI to be sent via a normal radio link usually permit MIDI signals to be stored on tape, and then played back again. Like a radio link, a cassette recorder or deck (even a good one) does not provide a wide enough bandwidth to permit MIDI signals to be stored and then retrieved in good enough condition to be decoded properly. The compression and expansion techniques again overcome this problem, enabling sequences to be stored on inexpensive audio cassettes.

There is at least one unit that is specifically designed to permit sequences to be stored on cassette tapes, and it provides some multi-tracking facilities. A system of this type has its attractions, and apart from enabling long sequences to be stored on a very low cost medium, it also has the advantage of being somewhat more portable than the average computer based system. It is also relatively cheap when compared to computer based or stand-alone real-time sequencers. There is a big disadvantage that the comprehensive editing facilities of computer and stand-alone units are not available on a tape based sequencer, even a sophisticated type. One of these units is perhaps best suited to those who are accomplished players who can usually get it right first time.

Finally

Quite a wide range of MIDI add-ons have been covered in this chapter, but there are probably many types, mainly of a highly specialised nature, that have not. If you are interested in this aspect of MIDI, and there are probably few MIDI users who would not benefit from using one or two MIDI gadgets, then it is well worth studying some catalogues and advertisements in electronic music magazines to find out what is available. Some of these units simply compensate for shortcomings in more major items of equipment, while others simply make life a little easier when using MIDI equipment. There is a more exciting category which enables MIDI to be used in more imaginative ways. It would be myopic to simply ignore these units and the possibilities that they open up.

5

General MIDI

The original MIDI specification was a very rigid framework which ensured that individual pieces of MIDI equipment could be used together to form a proper system. On the other hand, it did not lay down any minimum requirements for a MIDI system, and there were some aspects which were not regulated at all. In particular, no specific sounds, or even general types of sound, were assigned to program numbers. At the time the MIDI specification was formulated there was probably no great need to lay down any minimum requirements, or to assign standard sounds to program numbers. MIDI was designed as an interface that would enable users to build up music systems using equipment from several manufacturers. Users could simply slave one instrument to another, or build up a complex computer based sequencer system, depending on their needs and budget.

In the case of a sequencer based system there was no need for the MIDI specification to include standard sound assignments. Each user would know what sound or sounds were required for each channel of a sequence, because it was their own sequence. They would therefore know exactly how to set up their system to suit any sequence they would need to play back. Many users would be using sounds they had carefully fashioned themselves, and not "off the shelf" preset sounds. Having standard sound assignments would have been restrictive, and would have offered no obvious advantages.

Sound standards

It is probably fair to say that nothing has changed in this respect for the majority of MIDI users. When producing sequences most MIDI users simply assign any sound to any channel. The user knows which sound should be reproduced by each channel, and can soon set up the system to correctly play back a sequence. On the other hand, some users have found the need for a greater degree of standardisation than that set out in the original MIDI specification. It was probably the introduction of the standard MIDI file format that stimulated large scale interest in the idea of a fully standardised MIDI system.

Using standard MIDI sequencer files it is possible to take a sequence produced using one sequencer program, and play it back using any other sequencer that supports this file format. In theory it is even possible to produce a sequence using one computer, and then play it back on a different computer. For example, a sequence produced on an Atari ST based system could be played back on a PC based system. In practice there can be difficulties associated with this type of thing. These difficulties are generally more to do with incompatibilities between the different disk systems of the two computers, rather than any problem with MIDI itself. Provided any disk incompatibility problems can be overcome, the standard MIDI file format makes it possible for a wide range of MIDI users to swap music in the form of MIDI sequences.

Standard sequencer files make it easy to play back a sequence produced on one system using another, and completely different system, but they do not guarantee perfect results every time. Certain conditions must be met if a sequence is to be played back correctly. One obvious requirement is that any system used to play a MIDI sequence must have the wherewithal to reproduce it correctly. It is no good trying to play a 16 channel sequence that is polyphonic on all channels if all you have is a single instrument that provides monophonic operation on eight channels. Even if your system can play enough notes on a sufficient number of channels, can it respond to messages in the sequence such as aftertouch and pitchbend? If there is to be a large scale exchange of music in the form of MIDI sequences, it is clearly necessary for the sequences to be written for a fully standardised system that meets certain minimum requirements. A played back sequence will then include all the notes, and will have the right dynamic changes, etc.

The other requirement for sequences to be played back correctly is for each channel of the system to produce a suitable sound. Simply assigning a standard sound to each MIDI channel (e.g. violin on channel 1, piano on channel 2, etc.) is not a practical way of handling things. With only sixteen channels available this would limit a standard MIDI system to no more than sixteen different sounds, with the same sixteen sounds available for every piece. The more realistic approach is to have a standard set of sounds assigned to MIDI program numbers. This gives a much larger repertoire, with some 128 sounds available. In practice each standard sequencer file would then include a number of program changes at the beginning, and these would automatically select the right sound for each MIDI channel in use. Of course, if necessary further program change messages could be used mid-sequence, in order to switch channels to different sounds.

General MIDI

A relatively recent addition to the MIDI standard lays down the requirements for a standard MIDI system. The full title for this specification is "General MIDI System, Level 1", but it is better known as plain "General MIDI", or even just "GM" (which seems to have become something of a buzz-word in recent years). It is important to emphasise that General MIDI does not provide the specification for a system that all MIDI users should own. It simply sets out a specification for a system that can be used to play back standard MIDI sequencer files that are designed for use with a General MIDI system. If you do not wish to produce or play back standard sequencer files of this type, then you do not need a General MIDI system, and can continue to do your own thing. Of course, if you do wish to produce or play General MIDI sequencer files, then a MIDI system that rigidly conforms to the General MIDI standard is essential.

I suppose that any MIDI system which has the wherewithal could be set up to operate as a General MIDI system. If you need a General MIDI system, and your current equipment can be set up to provide the right sounds, etc., then there is little point in buying a General MIDI system. However, the basic idea of General MIDI is that sophisticated sound modules of the correct specification should be produced, giving non-technical users an off-the-shelf means of playing standard MIDI sequencer files. In fact it would be possible to produce complete

General MIDI players having built-in disk drives, amplifiers, and loud-speakers. MIDI files on computer disks could then be played as easily as playing an ordinary music cassette or a compact disc. As an alternative to computer disks, MIDI sequencer files could be distributed on compact discs. The amount of music that could be contained on each disc would be truly enormous.

Sound assignments

General MIDI is largely about the assignment of standard sounds to the 128 available program numbers. There is a slight complication in that there are two sets of sound assignments. These are so-called melodic sounds and the percussive types. The melodic sounds are those which have a definite pitch, and a pitch that can be controlled via MIDI note values. The percussive sounds are those which either do not have a definite pitch, or which do, but the pitch is fixed. For General MIDI purposes something like a steel drum sound would be a melodic sound not a percussion sound, because the pitch can be controlled via MIDI note values.

The normal way of handling percussion sounds is to allocate them their own channel, and this is the method used in General MIDI systems. This is more practical than having each percussion sound allocated to its own MIDI channel, which would often leave too few channels available for melodic sounds. Channel 10 has been assigned to percussion sounds, and a wide range of sounds are available. This works on the basis of having a different sound allocated to each note value, although not all of the 128 available values have been assigned a percussion sound. In fact, as yet, only note values from 35 to 81 have been assigned sounds, giving a repertoire of some 47 different percussive instruments. Possibly some of the other note values will eventually be given sound allocations. This would seem to be unlikely though, and it is probable that the high and low note values have been left unused due to the fact that many keyboard instruments can not generate note on/off messages containing these values. This could make it difficult to use them, although it is possible to edit note on/off messages to any desired value using most sequencers.

Following is a full list of the channel 10 allocations.

Channel 10 allocations

Prog	Sound	Prog	Sound
35	Acoustic bass drum	59	Ride cymbal 2
36	Bass drum 1	60	High bongo
37	Side stick	61	Low bongo
38	Acoustic snare	62	Mute hi conga
39	Hand clap	63	Open hi conga
40	Electric snare	64	Low conga
41	Low floor tom	65	High timbale
42	Closed hi-hat	66	Low timbale
43	High floor tom	67	High agogo
44	Pedal hi-hat	68	Low agogo 2
45	Low tom	69	Cabasa
46	Open hi-hat	70	Maracas
47	Low mid tom	71	Short whistle
48	High mid tom	72	Long whistle
49	Crash cymbal 1	73	Short guiro
50	High tom	74	Long guiro
51	Ride cymbal 1	75	Claves
52	Chinese cymbal	76	High woodblock
53	Ride bell	77	Low woodblock
54	Tambourine	78	Mute cuica
55	Splash cymbal	79	Open cuica
56	Cowbell	80	Mute triangle
57	Crash cymbal 2	81	Open triangle
58	Vibraslap		

All channels (apart from channel 10 of course) are available for melodic sounds. All 128 program numbers have been allocated melodic instrument sounds, and all fifteen channels must have all 128 of these available. The melodic sounds are divided into 16 groups with eight sounds in each group, as detailed below:

General MIDI sound assignment groups (not channel 10)

Program no	Group
1 – 8	Piano
9 – 16	Chromatic percussion
17 – 24	Organ
25 – 32	Guitar
33 – 40	Bass
41 – 48	Strings
49 – 56	Ensemble
57 – 64	Brass
65 – 72	Reed
73 – 80	Pipe
81 – 88	Synth lead
89 – 96	Synth pad
97 – 104	Synth effects
105 – 112	Ethnic
113 – 120	Percussive
121 – 128	Sound effects

General MIDI provides a wide range of sounds (see chart opposite), and it should be adequate in this respect for most users. It is only those who produce highly specialised types of music, or fairly avantgarde pieces, who are likely to find its repertoire of sounds too restricted. There is a potential problem with these standard sound assignments in that they are a bit vague. One manufacturer's idea of a bird tweet or violin sound is unlikely to be exactly matched by other manufacturers. Small variations from one instrument to another are not really of great importance, since there is some variation in the sounds of acoustic instruments of the same type. A sequence reproduced on two General MIDI sound modules will sound slightly different, but so would the same piece played by two different bands. Large differences in the sounds are a different matter though, and would make General MIDI rather pointless. The intention is that each sound should be more rigidly defined in the future, with parameters such as envelope attack and decay times being specified. This should avoid the situation where the same sequence played on two different General MIDI sound modules would sound substantially different.

Sound assignments (not channel 10)

Prog	Instrument	Prog	Instrument
1	Grand piano	37	Slap bass 1
2	Bright acoustic piano	38	Slap bass 2
3	Electric grand piano	39	Synth bass 1
4	Honky-tonk piano	40	Synth bass 2
5	Electric piano 1	41	Violin
6	Electric piano 2	42	Viola
7	Harpsichord	43	Cello
8	Clavi	44	Contrabass
9	Celesta	45	Tremolo strings
10	Glockenspiel	46	Pizzicato strings
11	Music box	47	Orchestral harp
12	Vibraphone	48	Timpani
13	Marimba	49	String ensemble 1
14	Xylophone	50	String ensemble 2
15	Tubular bells	51	Synth strings 1
16	Dulcimer	52	Synth strings 2
17	Drawbar organ	53	Choir aahs
18	Percussive organ	54	Voice oohs
19	Rock organ	55	Synth voice
20	Church organ	56	Orchestra hit
21	Reed organ	57	Trumpet
22	Accordion	58	Trombone
23	Harmonica	59	Tuba
24	Tango accordion	60	Muted trumpet
25	Acoustic gtr (nylon)	61	French horn
26	Acoustic gtr (steel)	62	Brass section
27	Electric guitar (jazz)	63	Synth brass 1
28	Electric guitar (clean)	64	Synth brass 2
29	Electric guitar (muted)	65	Soprano sax
30	Overdriven guitar	66	Alto sax
31	Distortion guitar	67	Tenor sax
32	Guitar harmonics	68	Baritone sax
33	Acoustic bass	69	Oboe
34	Electric bass (finger)	70	English horn
35	Electric bass (pick)	71	Bassoon
36	Fretless bass	72	Clarinet

Prog	Instrument	Prog	Instrument
73	Piccolo	101	FX 5 (brightness)
74	Flute	102	FX 6 (goblins)
75	Recorder	103	FX 7 (echoes)
76	Pan flute	104	FX 8 (sci-fi)
77	Blown bottle	105	Sitar
78	Shakuhachi	106	Banjo
79	Whistle	107	Shamisen
80	Ocarina	108	Koto
81	Lead 1 (square)	109	Kalimba
82	Lead 2 (sawtooth)	110	Bagpipe
83	Lead 3 (calliope)	111	Fiddle
84	Lead 4 (chiff)	112	Shanai
85	Lead 5 (charang)	113	Tinkle bell
86	Lead 6 (voice)	114	Agogo
87	Lead 7 (fifths)	115	Steel drums
88	Lead 8 (bass & lead)	116	Woodblock
89	Pad 1 (new age)	117	Taiko drum
90	Pad 2 (warm)	118	Melodic tom
91	Pad 3 (polysynth)	119	Synth drum
92	Pad 4 (choir)	120	Reverse cymbal
93	Pad 5 (bowed)	121	Guitar fret noise
94	Pad 6 (metallic)	122	Breath noise
95	Pad 7 (halo)	123	Seashore
96	Pad 8 (sweep)	124	Bird tweet
97	FX 1 (rain)	125	Telephone ring
98	FX 2 (soundtrack)	126	Helicopter
99	FX 3 (crystal)	127	Applause
100	FX 4 (atmosphere)	128	Gunshot

Making notes

General MIDI does not just define a standard set of sounds. It also sets certain minimum requirements for the number of voices, etc. Any sequence which is intended for use with a GM system must not exceed these minimum requirements. A GM system must be capable of providing 24 fully dynamically allocated voices. These should be simultaneously available for both melodic and percussive sounds. Alternatively, there should be 16 dynamically allocated voices available for melodic sounds, and eight available for percussive sounds. A GM system must be capable of operating on all sixteen MIDI channels. Rationalising things, this means that the instrument should be capable of sixteen note polyphonic, multi-timbral operation on MIDI channels 1 to 9, and 11 to 16, but it has to provide no more than sixteen notes at once across these channels. It must also be capable of providing up to eight percussion sounds simultaneously on channel 10. Clearly it is essential to take great care not to exceed these limits when producing a standard MIDI sequencer file which is intended for reproduction on a GM system.

All 128 program numbers must be implemented, as must all 128 of the instrument sounds, and all the percussion sounds. It is recommended that the instrument should be equipped with a master volume control, MIDI IN, OUT, and THRU sockets, plus stereo audio outputs and a headphone socket. These do not seem to be requirements, but a MIDI IN socket is clearly essential for playing back MIDI sequences unless the system has some form of built-in sequencer.

The General MIDI specification includes some further requirements governing the MIDI implementation. One of these requirements is that the instrument should have the correct octave registration (i.e. middle C should be at the correct note value of 60). This would seem to be a superfluous stipulation, but apparently some MIDI instruments provide the right notes but in the wrong octaves! This would not seem to fall within the normal MIDI specification anyway (except for out-of-range notes), but it is definitely not acceptable for a General MIDI system. All voices should respond to velocity information, and this includes the voice which provides the percussion sounds. Various MIDI control change messages must be implemented. These are:

Control no.	Controller
1	Modulation
7	Main volume
10	Pan
11	Expression
64	Sustain
121	Reset all controls
123	All notes off
Registered parameter numbers, 0, 1 and 2	

A General MIDI system should also respond to channel pressure messages (channel aftertouch) and pitch bend messages (with a default range of plus and minus two semitones).

At one time this sort of specification would have been a pretty tall order, and would probably have been implemented using several instruments. Using modern technology it is perfectly possible to implement this specification in a single MIDI sound generator module.

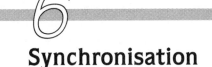

Synchronisation

There is a major category of MIDI gadget which comes under the general heading of synchronisation units. These fall into two sub-categories which are tape-to-MIDI synchronisers, and units for synchronising MIDI with drum machines that do not have a MIDI interface. Probably the tape synchronisers are the only type that are of interest to most MIDI users these days, but we will consider both types in this chapter, starting with the drum machine synchronisers.

Drum role

Drum machines in the pre MIDI era were generally synchronised with each other via a simple clock signal that consisted of a regular series of electrical pulses. With this system, like MIDI, one unit provides the synchronisation pulses, and all the other units lock onto this clock signal. Unlike MIDI, this system can not provide messages to do things like sending the sequencer to a particular point in the sequence and starting it there. The clock signal is started in order to begin a sequence, and switched off in order to stop a sequence. The individual units in the system must be manually set to the correct starting point (which usually entails nothing more than pressing a reset button). This system is a bit limited in scope, but it should be remembered that the integral sequencers of drum machines in the pre-MIDI era were generally of a much lower standard than those of today. They were generally programmed with nothing more than short repetitive tracks, and in most cases could not handle anything much beyond this.

It is possible to convert the pulsed clock signal from a drum machine into MIDI clock signals so that a MIDI sequencer can synchronise with the drum machine. It is more likely that the drum machine would be required to keep in synchronisation with the MIDI sequencer, and converters of this type have been produced. The number of clock pulses per quarter note is something that was not truly standardised in the pre-MIDI era. Some units used 24 pulses per quarter note, which matches MIDI's 24 clock messages per quarter note, but several other figures were used. For a successful conversion between MIDI and the old pulse synchronisation system, or vice versa, it is not essential for the pulse rate to match the MIDI clock rate. Modern electronics can easily handle a conversion from one pulse rate to another. Most practical synchronisers can handle several pulse rates.

Drum machines of the pre-MIDI era are now mostly unserviceable, or are still in full working order but have now have what is virtually museum piece status. Synchronisation units that will enable them to operate in MIDI systems are likely to prove difficult to obtain, and there is some doubt as to whether it is really worthwhile bothering with this type of thing any more. It might be better to spend the money on a good low cost drum machine of more recent origins. However, if you really need to synchronise a pre-MIDI drum machine to a MIDI system it can probably be done if you are prepared to spend some time seeking out a suitable synchroniser. This type of synchroniser is very easy to use. Simply couple the synchroniser's clock output to the clock input of the drum machine. The MIDI input of the synchroniser (and THRU socket if one is fitted) and then wired into the MIDI system just like any other MIDI slave device.

Getting it taped

The synchronisation units currently available are not, in the main, of the drum machine type, but are instead designed to synchronise MIDI systems with signals on magnetic recordings. These could be audio recordings, or possibly video recordings of some type. Either way the basic problem is much the same. The synchroniser must be able to convert MIDI clock signals into a form that can be stored on magnetic recording tape, and preferably on an ordinary audio track. It must also be able to take the data stored on the tape and turn it back into the appropriate MIDI messages. This is not a particularly straightforward job, since the bandwidth of an audio tape recording is inadequate to properly accommodate MIDI signals. However, with suitable signal processing and compression/expansion techniques it can be done. As we shall see later, not all synchronisers operate in precisely the manner described here, but instead use a slight variation on this scheme of things. This is to give compatibility with existing synchronisation standards.

I suppose that on the face of it the need for MIDI to tape synchronisation is not an obvious one. With a MIDI sequencer and a tape recorder set to suitable speeds, and started together, they should stay perfectly in synchronisation. In practice matters are not as straightforward as this. Even with only a very slight variation in the speed of one unit or the other, over a period of time they will slip significantly out of synchronisation (an effect known as "creeping sync". The speed stability of modern tape recorders is very good, but is not really good enough to guarantee that synchronisation will be properly maintained. The accuracy of a sequencer is potentially very good indeed, but with the microprocessor performing numerous background tasks such as keyboard scanning and display refreshing, it is difficult for a software writer to absolutely guarantee consistency in this respect.

If, for the moment, we assume that a sequencer and a tape recorder can be started together at the correct places, and will stay perfectly in synchronisation, this method of working lacks versatility. At a most basic level you can record all tracks on the sequencer, and then play and (or) sing along with them, recording everything onto tape. Synchronisation is then no problem, and it is simply up to the performers to stay in time with the played-back sequence. This is a perfectly valid approach, and one that may well be perfectly adequate, but if you change your mind about anything you will have to perform the piece again and record the new version. In theory you can record the live tracks one by one, and provided there are no creeping synchronisation problems this method will work perfectly. You can even go back and delete or add tracks on the sequencer. However, the editing of the sequence must not entail anything that will alter the tempo, as this would introduce a lack of synchronisation.

Unfortunately, this is a problem that persists even if any normal form of synchronisation is used. Although using a multi-track tape recorder with a MIDI system is often said to greatly increase the scope of the system, due to the tape recorder providing so-called "virtual tracks", things are not this simple in practice. Virtual tracks can greatly enhance a MIDI system, particularly if it is not equipped with banks of synthesisers to play all the MIDI tracks you may care to dream up. You should bear in mind though, that the virtual tracks cannot be edited in the same way as the data in MIDI tracks, and that the presence of tape tracks may prevent you from editing MIDI tracks in the way you would like.

Although fine in theory, the non-synchronised approach is probably not very practical. Apart from the likelihood of the sequencer and tape recorder tending to slip fractionally out of synchronisation, it is likely to be quite difficult to always get the two starting correctly in the right place. Quite small errors can stick out at least as prominently as the proverbial sore thumb. A synchroniser ensures that the sequencer will start at the right time, as well as keeping everything in perfect synchronisation until the end of the sequence. Even if you are not intending to do anything particularly clever, a tape synchroniser will usually make life very much easier. If you do wish to stretch the capabilities of a MIDI/tape system, a synchroniser will help you to do so, and will probably be an essential part of the system.

Double take

Apart from making any editing relatively easy and risk-free, a tape recorder plus synchroniser also enables the instruments in a system to be used more effectively. A big drawback of producing a piece as one huge MIDI sequence is that you then need a number sufficient instruments with enough voices to play the whole thing back, whether for a performance or to record the piece. You might not have enough instruments to handle this, or you might wish to mainly use the sounds of one instrument, which does not have enough voices to play all the parts allotted to it. With a synchroniser you can record some of the sounds onto tape tracks so that enough voices of the instruments are left free to play the MIDI sequence. Like conventional multi-track tape recording, you can use a single instrument to build up pieces as complex as you like.

As explained previously, the use of virtual tracks on tape brings the drawbacks of conventional tape multi-tracking, which mainly means a lack of ability to edit tracks recorded onto tape. However, this will often be a worthwhile trade-off, and you can always record the simple tracks on tape, with the more difficult ones being recorded in easy-editable form on the sequencer.

A synchroniser is not totally without drawbacks. Most obviously, it adds to the cost of the system. The cost of these units is not necessarily very high, but unless you really need to use a tape recorder and a MIDI sequencer side-by-side you might reasonably take the view that the money could be better spent on improving some other aspect of the system. Another drawback, albeit a minor one, is that the synchronisation signal occupies one track of the recorder, leaving one less for other purposes.

Tape sync types

A synchroniser is connected into the system in the manner shown in Figure 6.1. There are three basic types of synchroniser, and they are used in somewhat different ways. All types normally operate by putting what is called an f.s.k. (frequency shift keying) signal onto the tape. This means representing the two states of a digital signal by a low pitched tone and a high pitched one. In order to enable data to be

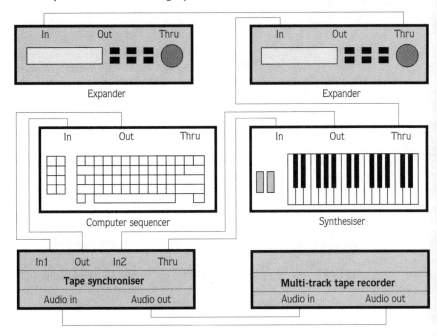

Figure 6.1 A typical setup using a tape synchroniser. The exact method of connection varies from one sync unit to another.

written onto the tape at a high rate it is actually a high pitched tone and an even higher pitched tone that are normally used in the current context. This gives a sort of high pitched warbling sound if you listen to an f.s.k. synchronisation track. Figure 6.2 shows the basic way in which a digital signal is encoded as an f.s.k. type.

In the most basic of units the information recorded onto the tape track is just basic MIDI start, clock and stop information. With these units there is no proper standardisation of the way information is coded onto the tape. This means that once you have recorded a synchronisation track onto tape you will probably be restricted to using the same synchroniser with that tape recording thereafter. A unit from a different manufacturer is unlikely to be able to decode the f.s.k. signal on the tape properly.

In use the sequencer is set to the mode where it generates MIDI clock signals, and it is then used to record the f.s.k. track (via the synchroniser) onto tape. This process is called "striping". In order to avoid crosstalk problems the f.s.k. signal is normally recorded on an outside track, and at the lowest level that will provide reliable results (usually about -10Vu). There should be a pilot tone to aid setting the required recording level. Systems that record digital data onto tape are not noted for their reliability, but after a little experimentation with recording levels it should be possible to obtain good reliability.

With the sequencer set to respond to external clock signals received via the MIDI input, the recorded f.s.k. signal is played back

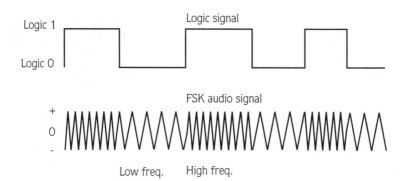

Figure 6.2 The sync signal is converted from a logic signal to an FSK type that can be recorded on tape, and decoded back to a logic signal on playback.

through the synchroniser and into the sequencer. It then produces MIDI timing signals that lock the sequencer to the tape recording, with any very slight variations in the speed of the tape recorder producing identical fluctuations in the tempo of the sequencer. This keeps the two perfectly in synchronisation.

With this type of synchroniser you must start by producing all the tracks in the sequencer, or at least a fair percentage of them, complete with any variations in tempo. Remember that once you have striped the tape and started recording audio tracks onto it, you can not alter the tempo in the sequencer. Any attempt to do so will not result in a loss of synchronisation. Instead, the sequencer will still lock onto the clock signals from the tape, and no change in tempo will be obtained. The timing information on the tape effectively overrides some of the editing facilities of the sequencer, making it advisable to get the whole sequence rather than just some of the sequencer tracks perfected before striping the tape. This is a factor that is common to any setup that has the sequencer responding to an external clock signal. Where possible it is usually best to have other devices synchronised to the sequencer, rather than the sequencer synchronised to some other device in the system. In this case there is no easy way of synchronising the tape recorder to the sequencer, and so the sequencer has to be synchronised to the recorder.

Another limitation of this method of synchronisation is that the timing information stored on tape is just start, stop, and clock signals. There are no song position pointer messages to permit a sequence to be started somewhere in the middle. You must always start the tape from the beginning so that the sequencer receives a start message, followed by the clock signals which synchronise it to the tape as the sequence progresses. With short sequences this might not matter, or every track might be full from the beginning to the end of the piece anyway. In real life though, you will often wish to start mid-sequence, and having to play sequences from the beginning each time can waste a great deal of time (as well as being more than a little irksome).

Adding a merger

A MIDI merge unit can be a useful accessory when using a tape synchroniser. If you complete the MIDI sequence and then add the audio tracks there is no problem. Should you wish to go back and add or replace a track on the sequencer once work has started on the audio tracks on tape, there is the likely problem of two MIDI outputs to feed into one MIDI input. In other words, the synchroniser must still feed into the input of the sequencer in order to regulate the tempo, but you will probably need to connect a keyboard or other control device here as well so that the new track can be played into the sequencer. This requires the use of a proper merge unit that will give a valid output when fed with simultaneous input signals. No form of MIDI switcher will give the desired effect. A typical setup using a synchroniser plus merge unit is shown in Figure 6.3. In some cases the synchroniser pro-

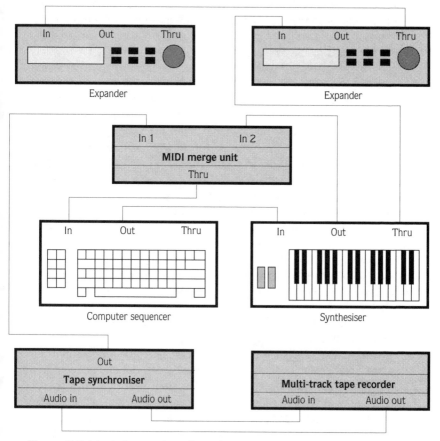

Figure 6.3 A typical sync setup where the sync unit has no built-in merge facility.

vides a built-in merge facility, which is more than a little helpful. Some sequencers have a built-in tape synchroniser, and a unit of this type should be able to handle simultaneous input from the tape recorder and a keyboard or other MIDI control device.

Time coding

The other two types of tape synchroniser use some form of time coding, or a sort of pseudo time coding. This can either be the standard SMPTE (Society of Motion Picture Technicians and Engineers, and normally pronounced something like sumpty or simpty), or a unique method of coding devised by the manufacturer. The SMPTE code is well established, having originally been devised in 1967 (which means that it predates MIDI by many years). A time coded system like SMPTE does not just use a series of clock signals on the tape, but puts down a series of times. The SMPTE code was originally intended primarily for use in audio/visual systems, especially television. Its time coding therefore operates on the basis of hours, minutes, seconds, frames, and sub-frames (80 sub-frames per frame). Matters are complicated by the fact that SMPTE can operate with several frame rates. These rates are 25 fps (frames per second) for European television, 30 frames per second for American television (or 29.7 fps for the drop-frame system), and 24 fps for film use.

Probably most MIDI users will use their systems only in conjunction with audio tape equipment, and it is then of no importance which system is used. With an audio only system there are no frames to worry about, and the synchronisation track carries what effectively becomes straightforward timing information in twenty fifths of a second, or whatever the frame rate dictates. I suppose that for UK users a frame rate of 25 per second is the most sensible choice, since this will provide compatibility with European video systems if they should ever progress into the audio/visual field.

With a SMPTE system the synchroniser has to be a very sophisticated piece of electronics since there is no easy correlation between the SMPTE time code and the normal MIDI system real-time messages. There are now MIDI time code (MTC) messages which can slightly simplify matters, and these are described in detail at the end of this chapter.

MIDI timing messages do not have to be converted into corresponding SMPTE codes when striping a tape. The synchroniser itself generates the necessary timing signals. This is clearly a fundamental difference between the simple clock-type synchronisers described previously, and the time code variety. The SMPTE timing signals do have to be converted into MIDI messages when the tape is played back. This complex process is usually handled by a microprocessor in the synchroniser. Units of this type normally have some ability to utilise MIDI song position pointer or MTC messages, so that you do not always have to record each audio track right from the beginning of the piece.

It is perhaps worth pointing out that some tape synchronisers interface direct onto the data bus of the microprocessor, rather than going via the MIDI ports. This eases the task of the microprocessor slightly, but this approach is only feasible when using a tape synchroniser and sequencer program/computer (or dedicated sequencer unit) that are designed to work together. When using a synchroniser of this type it will not be connected in the manner described here, but it should be supplied with an instruction manual that makes the correct method of interconnection perfectly clear.

In use, the first task is usually to record the SMPTE track for a length of time that is comfortably longer than the sequence. This differs from the way in which simple f.s.k. synchronisers are used, where at least one track in the sequencer would normally be produced first, so that there is some timing information (complete with any required tempo variations), to place onto the tape. The SMPTE signal is a straightforward high resolution timing type which is always the same, and does not vary in sympathy with any changes in the tempo of recorded sequencer tracks. The synchronisation is obtained on the basis of the sequencer reading the time code information which it uses to go to the correct beat in the appropriate bar. If the tape should speed up, then the time codes will be received slightly prematurely, and the sequencer will speed up so that it stays in synchronisation with the tape recorder. Similarly, if the tape recorder should slow down, the timing signals will be received slightly late, causing the sequencer to slow down and stay in synchronisation.

On the face of it the sequencer is locked onto the strict timing of the SMPTE track, which will be reflected in musicbox style tracks having perfect and emotionless timing. In reality, unless excessive quantisation is used (which would give this effect anyway), the sequencer will not rigidly regulate note timing in this fashion. It should not do this when any form of time code synchronisation is used, allowing full freedom of expression with no quantisation at all if desired. This is all dependent on the sequencer program though, and is not something that is influenced by the synchroniser.

The piece will not normally start at the beginning of the time code track, but after a lead-in of perhaps ten seconds. The synchroniser will probably enable the start point to be specified. The time signature of the piece will need to be entered into the synchroniser to aid the SMPTE to MIDI timing conversion. Often there is a multi-digit display which shows the SMPTE time and frame count, or it might show MIDI bar numbers. With a time code synchronisation system you can produce the MIDI sequencer tracks and the tape tracks in any order you like. However, as already pointed out, once you have produced some tape tracks your MIDI editing options are likely to be reduced somewhat. My preference would be to add the tape tracks as late in the process as possible. Of course, if you are doing something like producing MIDI sequences to accompany an audio/visual presentation, you will probably not have any choice about the order of things. The MIDI sequence must be tailored to suit the existing program material on tape, and your hands are tied in this respect.

Pseudo time code

Rather than use SMPTE time code, some synchroniser manufacturers have opted for time coding of their own design. This permits sophisticated features to be included in the system with relative ease. Like simple clock signal style tape synchronisation, the lack of standardisation with this method means that the synchronisation track on the tape will probably only be usable with one particular model of synchroniser. This could give problems at a later date when you have moved on to a different synchroniser, although the new unit might have so-called "backwards compatibility" with the old unit. By then you might have mixed down all the tape and sequencer tracks into completed tape recordings of each piece, and there would then be no further need to synchronise the tapes. This rather leaves your options closed though. The importance of all this, or lack of it, is something you have to assess for yourself, and it is obviously dependent on the way you work and the type of thing you undertake with the equipment.

Most of these proprietary time codes are not, strictly speaking, time codes. With a true time code there is only a series of times placed onto the tape, with absolute regularity. There is no MIDI to SMPTE conversion, only a conversion in the opposite direction. For many purposes there is something to be said for a system which deals in MIDI clock signals, but with the refinement of song position pointers being included as well. A unit that took MIDI timing signals, recorded them on tape as a series of clock and song position messages stored in an f.s.k. coded form, and then converted them back into MIDI messages on playback, would be very useful. It would be used much like a simple clock signal type synchroniser, with at least one MIDI track being recorded first in order to generate some meaningful timing information that could be stored on tape. Such a unit would have the advantage over simple clock signal synchronisers that if the tape was started in the middle of a piece, the song position pointer messages would enable the sequencer to quickly jump to the correct point in the sequence and synchronise correctly.

Most of the up-market non-SMPTE synchronisers do seem to adopt this approach to the problem, rather than a true time coding system. In terms of the facilities offered they are often similar to SMPTE units, but they should be regarded as improved clock signal synchronisers as they are used as such. With some units you might have to provide information such as the time signature, but this will probably only be to ensure that a bar count display or something of this type keeps count correctly. Giving the wrong time signature would probably not stop the system from working, apart from the display giving the wrong count of course.

Bear in mind that if you start somewhere in the middle of a piece, neither the synchroniser or the sequencer will be able to instantly jump to the correct point in the sequence. The sequencer will probably take about a second, or possibly two, to correctly lock onto the signal from the tape recorder. There is probably a greater variation with sequencers, and the time taken for a sequencer to respond to a song position pointer is often heavily dependent on the amount of data that has been stored in the unit. It could be as much as a few seconds. Obviously the tape should be started at least a few seconds ahead of the starting point for the track, so that the synchroniser and sequencer have time to lock on properly before this point is reached.

Extras

With some tape synchronisers you get one or two useful additional features. The inclusion of a merge facility, and its usefulness have been mentioned previously. A built-in MIDI merge facility is probably the most useful "extra" that a tape synchroniser can have. Fortunately, this seems to be a very common feature, but it is by no means a universal one. When comparing prices, remember that a bargain unit that does not have an integral merge facility might not be such a bargain if you have to buy a merge unit before you can use it properly.

Some SMPTE types have an audio input which is intended to permit synchronisation to a live player, or to a source on tape. The SMPTE track is placed on tape in the normal way, or possibly on a tape which has already been recorded with some music tracks. On playback, the MIDI signals are derived from the SMPTE code and the live input fed to the audio input from a suitable electronic instrument (or from a tape track). This has its uses, but may not be easy to use effectively in practice. It is perhaps something of a love it or hate it feature.

In common with other electronic music devices, the more complex synchronisers usually have some means of storing sets of control settings externally for quick and easy recall later. This might be in the form of a system exclusive dump via MIDI to a suitable storage device, which is usually a computer running a suitable program. Alternatively, there may be the option to dump data onto tape. The latter is possibly the more convenient, since you will certainly have a tape deck for storage of the data, but you might not have anything that can store and retrieve system exclusive dumps properly. On the other hand, tape dump systems have gained a reputation for being about as reliable as computer cassette interfaces. In other words, they tend to be regarded by many as worse than useless. This reputation is probably not fully justified, but systems for storing this type of data on tape do tend to be something less than foolproof. Usually some experimentation with recording level settings will produce reliable results, and provided you make a note of the optimum recording level for future use, there should be no major difficulties.

Right choice

When choosing a tape synchroniser you need to give careful thought to the manner in which the unit will be used. In general, if you have no real need for SMPTE compatibility, an SMPTE unit will probably not represent the best value for money. It might not represent a particularly easy way of achieving the desired effect either. These units tend to be slightly less straightforward to use than the non-SMPTE types. On the other hand, some SMPTE synchronisers at reasonable prices do now seem to be available. If there is a SMPTE synchroniser that is specifically designed for your particular sequencer, and its cost is reasonable, the support offered by the sequencer for this particular synchroniser might make it the obvious choice.

If SMPTE compatibility is not of any importance, then even a simple MIDI clock type synchroniser will probably do the job quite well. Unless you are going to produce only short sequences, a more sophisticated unit that supports song position pointers or MTC is likely to be worth the extra cost though, provided you can find one at a reasonable price. This should not be too difficult these days. All the non-SMPTE synchronisers seem to be relatively low cost types, and virtually all now offer something beyond basic clock signal synchronisation.

MTC

The original MIDI specification did not include any special timing messages to make it relatively easy to use a MIDI system with SMPTE tape system. The only way of integrating the two types of system was by converting timing information from the SMPTE system into MIDI clock messages, song position pointer messages, etc. This is possible, but is relatively difficult. Eventually some special timing messages were introduced into the MIDI specification, and these are the MIDI time code (MTC) messages. Apart from making it easier for the two types of system to operate together, MTC should also enable them to operate in a slightly more sophisticated fashion.

MIDI time code is basically just a string of messages which give the position in a sequence in terms of hours, minutes, seconds, and frames. In other words, using exactly the same method of timing as used in the SMPTE system. The main MIDI time code message is the MTC quarter frame type, which is a system common message. There are eight different MTC quarter frame messages, with each one providing part of the elapsed time. A set of eight MTC quarter frame messages are needed in order to provide the slave sequencer with a complete time. Each of these messages is a two byte type. The status byte has the system message code (1111 in binary) in its most significant nibble, and the MTC quarter frame code (0001 in binary) in its least significant nibble.

The data byte has two functions, one of which is to indicate which part of the time it is carrying (frame, seconds, minutes, or hours). This operates on the basis of having the most significant nibble indicate which part of the time the message carries, with the least significant nibble holding the actual data. There is a slight problem with this arrangement in that it provides only four bits of data per message, which is not enough for any part of the time. The hours, minutes, and seconds count runs from 0 to 59 and the frame count runs from 0 to 29. Four bits of data provide a range of just 0 to 15 (decimal). Each part of the time therefore has to be carried by two MIDI messages, and it is for this reason that eight rather than four messages are needed in order to send a complete time. The most significant bit of the data byte is always set to 0, leaving three bits to indicate which part of the time the message is providing. This is just sufficient to accommodate the eight different types of MTC quarter frame message.

This table shows the way in which the MTC quarter frame messages are coded.

MTC message no.	Value carried In data nibble
0	Frame count, LS nibble
1	Frame count, MS nibble
2	Seconds count, LS nibble
3	Seconds count, MS nibble
4	Minutes count, LS nibble
5	Minutes count, MS nibble
6	Hours count, LS nibble
7	Hours count, MS nibble

Unused data bits are set to 0 by the sending device, and are simply ignored by the receiving device. The slave sequencer can not achieve lock until it has received a full set of eight MTC messages. These messages are sent only when the system is running (unlike ordinary MIDI clock signals which can be sent continuously). Even if superfluous messages are avoided, and only parts of the time that have actually changed are updated, it still takes a fair number of MIDI messages per second in order to keep the two systems accurately locked. However, it apparently takes less than 10% of MIDI's capacity to keep everything working properly, leaving plenty of room for other MIDI messages to be fitted in. In practice this is probably irrelevant, as it is unlikely that these messages would be sent together with general MIDI activity. Incidentally, they are called quarter frame messages because they are sent at a rate of four per frame (two frames per complete set of eight digits). Figure 6.4 shows a four byte sequence that sets the seconds count at 36 seconds.

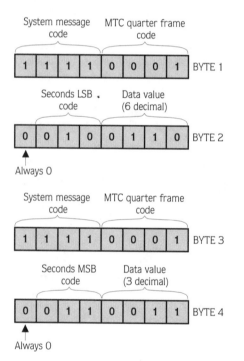

Figure 6.4 Two MTC messages which set the seconds count at 36 seconds.

There is actually rather more to MTC than the quarter frame messages. Further messages can be sent in the form of universal system exclusive messages (see Chapter 8). One of these is the "full message", which is a ten byte sequence that contains the full time. The general idea is that the quarter frame messages should be used during the normal operation of the system, but full messages should be used when the system is in the fast-forward or rewind mode. Simply sending normal quarter frame messages at a high rate is not a very practical way of handling things. Instead, a full message is sent, and the slave sequencer moves to the specified time. It then pauses at that position in the sequence until it is restarted by an ordinary quarter frame message.

A further universal system exclusive message can handle up to 32 "user bits". These bits can be used for special purposes, but their exact function and method of coding varies from system to system (if they are implemented at all). There is also a 13 byte universal system exclusive message which can be used to implement MIDI cueing.

7

MIDI programming

I think it is safe to assume that most users of MIDI who own a computer are more interested in using ready-made applications software than writing their own programs. This seems to be a realistic attitude, since writing computer software is a fairly involved and specialist task. On the other hand, many people who own computers, including those who have bought them primarily for MIDI purposes, have some programming knowledge which could occasionally be put to good use in a MIDI context.

I would certainly not urge the writing of complex software such as a sequencer. If all you need is something pretty basic, then I suppose a simple do-it-yourself sequencer might be a practical proposition. Even for something of this type, you might find that there is some public domain software that suits your requirements quite well, and is available at very low cost. Competing with sophisticated commercial software is not a very practical proposition. The top music software is written by full-time professional programmers who are very expert at their job, and can put a massive amount of man hours into the task. In fact some of the more complicated software takes man years rather than man hours in order to get everything fully perfected and debugged. Even if you have the programming skills, you are unlikely to have enough time to write complex music software that genuinely achieves professional standards.

Utilities

A more effective way of using part time programming skills in a MIDI context is to write your own utility software. Here we are talking in terms of programs such as MIDI monitors for testing suspect MIDI equipment, and MIDI processing such as channelising. There is a problem in using a computer in this way in that you may often wish to have the computer running a sequencer or other major piece of software, and providing some MIDI monitoring or processing task. With most computers (in fact all the ones I have encountered) there is no way of doing this. However, when the computer is not needed for other purposes, it can often be gainfully utilised in monitoring and processing applications. Also, if you upgrade to a new computer, and retain the old one, you may well find that the old computer can be used as a very effective MIDI processor, possibly giving facilities of a type that are only matched by quite expensive dedicated MIDI processing units.

Obviously this type of programming is in many respects like any other type of programming, making use of the usual loops, conditional tests, printing to screen, etc. There are some ways in which MIDI programming differs from most other types of programming though, and we will concentrate on these differences rather than trying to make this chapter a general discussion of programming techniques. With a substantial number of different computers currently in common use in MIDI systems, it is possible here only to cover the subject in general terms. It must be assumed that you are familiar with programming your computer in at least one common programming language, and also have some knowledge about accessing the MIDI ports. If you do not, then it is only fair to point out that you will probably not benefit a great deal from reading this chapter.

Having the necessary technical know-how to access the MIDI port properly is an important factor, since accessing MIDI ports is often something less than completely straightforward. In fact it involves some convoluted programming in some cases. Matters are likely to be most easy with a computer that has built-in MIDI ports. The computer's firmware (i.e. its built-in operating system software) should then provide some routines to simplify access to the MIDI ports. As MIDI is a rather specialised interface, a set of MIDI ports is not included as standard on many computers. It is to be found on the Atari ST range of computers (which are very popular with MIDI users), plus a few others, including some of the more recent Atari machines.

Integral MIDI

Where a MIDI interface is fitted as standard, any high level programming language for the computer should provide a means of
accessing it. With the Atari STs for instance, the MIDI interface is port
number 3 when both reading or writing data. In ST BASIC it can be
accessed using the INP and OUT functions (e.g. PRINT INP 3 and OUT
3,127). Other high level languages for the ST should provide some
similar means for accessing the port, and even low level languages are
likely to have some relatively easy way of linking to the in-built support
routines for the MIDI port.

Apart from having a definite means of sending data to and reading it from the MIDI port, there is another advantage in having a built-in
MIDI interface. The commands that send data to or collect data from
the port are sophisticated routines that handle the flow of data correctly. If you send large amounts of data to the port in rapid succession,
you will not lose data due to one byte being received before the existing
one has been transmitted. A small section of memory (usually about
128 to 512 bytes) will be set aside to act as a buffer. In other words,
if data is sent to the port too quickly, excess bytes are stored in the
buffer until they can be sent. Obviously data could be sent to the port at
such a rate that the buffer would become overloaded, but this is not
likely to occur in practice. For this to happen there would have to be a
severe case of MIDI choke, and some sort of malfunction would
become almost inevitable anyway. The routines controlling the correct
flow of data to the port, via the buffer if necessary, are "invisible" to
the user. You just send data to the port as and when necessary, and
leave it to the computer to ensure that the flow of data is regulated
properly.

There will also be routines to ensure that data can be read
from the MIDI port without the danger of any missed bytes. This is
more important than having routines to control things in the opposite
direction, since reading a MIDI port is potentially a difficult problem.
You have to bear in mind that MIDI bytes are often sent end-to-end. As
soon as one byte (complete with its stop bit) has been sent, the next
byte will commence. With a baud rate of 31250, and a total of ten
bits per byte (including the start and stop bits), this works out at about
3125 bytes per second, or only something in the region of 0.3 milliseconds per byte. Some languages are faster than others, but with one of
the slower high level languages, such as an interpreted BASIC, it may

well be impossible to read the port at a fast enough rate to avoid missing bytes. In an extreme case you might only read something like every tenth byte!

The situation is made worse by the fact that it is not just a matter of reading the port, you must first ensure that there is a new byte of data to be processed. Otherwise it is a virtual certainty that there will be multiple readings of many bytes, giving unusable results. Multiple readings are normally avoided by monitoring the appropriate bit of a status register in the MIDI interface device, and only reading the port when this bit of the register is set to 1. Most "flags" of this type are automatically reset when data is read from the device, but in some cases a certain value must be written to the appropriate register in order to reset the flag. A single read cycle would therefore consist of a loop to repeatedly read and test the data ready flag bit, with the data register being read only when a positive result was obtained from the test. Then, if necessary, the data ready flag would be reset by a suitable write instruction to its control register.

With data bytes being received at only about 0.3 millisecond intervals on occasions, the computer must obviously be able to undertake instructions at a rate of at least a few thousand per second in order to guarantee that this sort of thing can be carried out reliably. A slow BASIC will be about ten times too slow. One of the faster interpreted BASICs might be able to handle the task, but probably only just. A fast language, such as a compiled BASIC, or virtually any compiled language come to that, should be able to handle the task. An assembly language or machine code routine, even on a fairly slow computer, should also be able to handle this sort of processing. Remember that machine code routines are easily accessed by most BASICs, and that you will not necessarily be faced with the task of writing the whole program in machine code in order to obtain fast enough operation. On the other hand, some MIDI processing tasks are very simple, and are not that difficult to write in machine code or assembly language.

Please interrupt

Even when using a programming language that is suitably fast, there is still a danger of MIDI data not being read reliably, with the odd byte or two tending to go absent without leave occasionally. This can even happen when using assembly language or machine code routines, which are capable of operating at speeds which should, on the face of it, be easily high enough to ensure reliable results. The cause of the problem is interrupts. This is a facility provided by all the microprocessors I have come across, and something that is exploited to the full in most computers. In fact it is something that is possibly slightly overdone in some computers.

The basic idea is to have some extra inputs on the microprocessor, appropriately called the interrupt inputs. A peripheral device of some kind can indicate to the microprocessor that it needs urgent attention by signalling via its interrupt input. The microprocessor then breaks out of the task it is currently undertaking, services the device that has generated the interrupt, and then returns to its original task to continue where it left off.

The interrupt generating devices have a hierarchy that gives precedence to those circuits which have the most urgent needs. This helps to avoid having a really urgent task held up while a less urgent interrupt driven task is carried out. In many computers there are a large number of interrupt generating circuits, including such things as ports, the display driver circuit, and timers. The problem with this system is that while your program is monitoring and reading the MIDI input, the computer will be continuously breaking out of your routine and into numerous interrupt driven routines. Interrupt routines are normally kept quite short, and this system is usually reliant on the routines being kept very brief. This means that the odd interrupt during your MIDI port reading routine is unlikely to cause any problems, even if it should occur at just the wrong time.

This can not be guaranteed though, and some computers possible have interrupt routines that are sufficiently long to cause difficulties. The main problem is that with a number of peripheral circuits generating interrupts at different frequencies, there will sometimes be two or more interrupts in rapid succession. This can produce a relatively long break in your MIDI port reading routine, causing bytes to be missed, apparently at random.

With an integral MIDI port this problem should not occur, since the port itself will be an interrupt generating circuit. It should be given sufficient precedence to ensure that it does not get interrupted for so long that bytes of data are missed. Some add-on MIDI interfaces are quite sophisticated, and give some help to the programmer. There may even be software routines supplied with the interface (possibly in a

ROM device that is part of the interface), to make using the unit as straightforward as using a built-in type. Most computers are designed in such a way that external add-ons can generate interrupts, and a sophisticated MIDI interface is likely to make use of any interrupt facility that is available.

With a computers such as the Commodore Amiga range, where the MIDI interface is an add-on that fits onto the serial port, you have what is virtually a built-in MIDI port. Having set the correct baud rate, you then read from and write to the serial port, which effectively becomes the MIDI port. The computer and any high level languages designed to run on it should provide support for the serial port in much the same way that support is provided for a built-in MIDI port.

If your computer has only a very simple MIDI interface you might find that writing software to read from it reliably is quite tricky. Writing data to the port is not likely to be too difficult, and entails little more than POKEing values to the appropriate address, or whatever. You need to be careful not to send data at an excessive rate when using a language that is sufficiently fast to do this. Many interpreted BASICs are not fast enough to overload the interface, but the faster ones running on 16 bit computers might do so. Most compiled languages (plus assembly language and machine code routines) are almost certain to overload the interface unless steps are taken to avoid this. The most simple solution is to use a timing loop between multiple write operations to the port. A little experimentation should soon reveal a suitable number of loops for a simple delay loop routine.

Alternatively, there should be a flag in the status register of the interface device that can be monitored. This will go to logic 1 when the device is ready to receive a fresh byte of data. This enables the flow of data into the port to be regulated by checking the state of this flag, and repeatedly rechecking it if necessary, and only writing a byte of data to the port when the flag is at the logic 1 state.

Don't interrupt

Reading the port is likely to prove problematic for the reasons already discussed. If you use a fast programming language (preferably machine code or assembler), and the computer does not make extensive use of interrupts, there may be no problems. My experiences would tend to suggest that this is unlikely though. I have tried using

assembly language routines to access simple MIDI ports on three different makes of computer, and in all three cases there were reliability
problems. Sometimes the problem will be severe, with bytes tending to
be missed even if MIDI messages are fed to the port at a fairly low
rate. With other computers the problem may only arise if data is supplied to the port at a fairly high rate. You might find that a monophonic
input can be read correctly, or possibly even three note chords, but
four notes or more at a time causes bytes to be missed.

The usual solution to the problem is to disable interrupts. You
can not usually do this on the basis of simply switching off all interrupts
permanently. This might actually be possible in some cases, but will
result in certain facilities of the computer (timers and the display perhaps) becoming inoperative. At least one or two interrupt routines will
almost certainly be essential to the correct functioning of the computer, and switching them off will then simply result in the computer
crashing.

There are two basic approaches to the problem. With many
computers you have the option of selectively switching off interrupts.
You may be able to control the ability of individual devices to generate
interrupts, but matters are often less precise than this. As pointed out
previously, interrupts normally operate on a hierarchical basis. You can
often block interrupts that are below a certain level of importance.
With a little experimentation it is often possible to find a blocking level
that enables the MIDI port to be read reliably, but which does not result
in the computer hanging up.

The second approach is to disable all interrupts, but not permanently. This could operate on the basis of disabling interrupts when a
new byte of data is detected, and enabling them again when this byte,
plus any received immediately afterwards, have been processed. This
method is likely to be less satisfactory, since an interrupt might be generated after the presence of a fresh byte of data has been detected,
but before the program gets a chance to disable interrupts. Also, by
switching off interrupts you are not preventing routines from being carried out. As soon as interrupts are re-enabled, any outstanding interrupt calls will be serviced in their hierarchical order. By disabling interrupts for a short period of time you might be storing up trouble, which
will produce a malfunction if a fresh set of data is received very soon
after the previous batch. Ideally a MIDI interface should be able to generate interrupts so that it can be given the precedence it deserves.

Bit by bit

With most programming there is no need to deal with anything less than complete bytes, but the situation is different with MIDI programming. Often the program has to operate on just a few bits of each byte, or possibly just one bit. In particular, when reading status flags, and when processing MIDI header bytes, it can often be important to read the state of just one bit, or perhaps three or four bits of a byte.

A microprocessor does provide facilities for reading bytes on a bit by bit basis, but only in round about fashions. Some instructions are conditional on the setting of one bit of the byte being tested, and this is usually the most or least significant bit. But what if the bit you wish to test is not the most or least significant one? You simply use rotate or shift instructions to move the appropriate bit into a position in the byte where it can be tested. Several bits can be tested using a series of rotate or shift instructions, with a conditional instruction being used between each one. This is a rather cumbersome way of handling the task though, and not one that I would recommend. Anyway, it is only applicable when using assembly language or machine code and is not a facility that is likely to be found in many high level languages.

An easier way, and one that is possible using most computer languages, is to use bitwise ANDing. You need to be a little careful here, because the AND instruction in some computer languages (particularly BASICs) does not operate in the required bitwise manner. If it does not, there may well be a bitwise AND function under a different name, such as BAND. Most high level languages have a bitwise AND function, and all microprocessors seem to have bitwise AND instructions. Consequently, in the unlikely event that the high level language you are using does not support this function, it should still be available using a machine code or assembly language routine.

If you get the computer to bitwise AND a couple of numbers chosen at random, the result may seem rather strange. If you try this a few times you could reasonably come to the conclusion that the answers are every bit as random as the two numbers being processed, with no logic in the answer at all. Consider these examples:

```
   27 AND 198 = 2
  123 AND 255 = 123
  123 AND 123 = 123
  123 AND 0   = 0
   85 AND 67  = 65
```

There is no obvious connection between the two numbers being ANDed and the answer, and the only overall feature you might notice is that the answer is never larger than the smaller of the two numbers being processed. Strangely, ANDing a number with two different numbers can give identical answers! In the examples above, ANDing 123 with 255 and 123 gave an answer of 123 in both cases.

In order to understand bitwise AND operations you have to consider numbers in their binary form. This is the 85 AND 67 = 65 example in its binary form:

01010101 AND 01000011 = 01000001

When considering the ANDing process it is actually much easier if the numbers are stacked vertically, as here.

First number   01010101
Second number   01000011
Answer   01000001

This shows how simple the process really is. If you consider things on a column by column basis, you will notice that if there are two 0s or a 1 and a 0 in the top two lines, then there is a 0 in that column of the answer. A 1 only appears in a column of the answer if there is a 1 in that column for both the numbers being processed. This may seem a bit clever but rather useless in practice, but it is something that is crucial to much MIDI programming. By ANDing MIDI bytes with a suitable number, you can mask off some bits and read others. Use a 0 in the masking number for bits you wish to mask off, and a 1 for bits you wish to read.

As a simple example, suppose that we require a test that will show whether received bytes are header or data types. We need to read the most significant bit, which is 1 for header bytes and 0 for data bytes. The masking number would therefore be 10000000 in binary, or 128 in decimal. The answer will then be 10000000 in binary (128 decimal) if the tested byte is a header type, or 00000000 in binary (0 in decimal) if it is a data byte. These two examples show how this works

First number (data)	01000100
Mask	10000000
Answer	00000000

First number (header)	10010101
Mask	10000000
Answer	10000000

In a MIDI context it is often necessary to test several bits, and not just one. Suppose that we need a routine to not only sort out the header bytes from the data bytes, but to also reveal the channel number of the message. This can be achieved by first using the process described previously to sort out the header bytes, and then ANDing these bytes with a mask number of 00001111 (15 in decimal). These examples show how this provides the desired result.

Header byte	10010011
Mask	00001111
Answer	00000011

Header byte	10111111
Mask	00001111
Answer	00001111

In the first example the answer is 00000011 in binary, which is the equivalent of 3 in decimal numbers. Remember that the value in the channel nibble is actually one less than the MIDI channel number, and this message is therefore on channel 4. Similarly, in the second example the channel value is 00001111 in binary, or 15 in decimal, which means that it is actually the header byte for a channel 16 message.

You need to be careful when processing MIDI data, as the intricacies of MIDI can sometimes lead you into difficulties. In this example we seem to be sorting out status bytes all right, and then extracting the channel number in the required way. However, not all MIDI messages are channel types, and we might actually be extracting the message type nibble from a system message, rather than the channel number from a channel type. In order to ensure that this did not happen it would be necessary to adopt a three stage test. The first test would be to sort out status bytes from data bytes. The next test would be to check for the system message header byte (11110000 in binary, or 240 in decimal). Bytes that failed this second test would then be given the third stage of processing, which is to extract the channel number. ANDing using a mask number of 11110000 in binary (240 in decimal) will sort out system messages from channel types. If the answer is 240, then the header byte is that of a system message. Any other value and it is the header byte of a channel message. These examples shows how this masking number provides the desired effect.

Note on header	10010101
Mask	11110000
Answer	10010000
MIDI clock header	11111000
Mask	11110000
Answer	11110000
Note off header	10001111
Mask	11110000
Answer	10000000

Filtering

As a simple example of a program to provide simple MIDI pro-cessing, assume that we wish to use an Atari ST computer as a filter to remove MIDI clock signals. This simple four line Fast BASIC program will do the job.

```
REPEAT
X = INP(3)
IF (X AND 255) < > 248 THEN OUT 3,X
UNTIL FALSE
```

This uses a REPEAT... UNTIL loop to make the program repeat indefinitely, but obviously other types of loop could be used here, including an old style BASIC GOTO if nothing better is available. The second line reads in a byte of data from the MIDI port and places it in variable "X". Having a built-in MIDI port that is supported by the programming language makes this task very much easier, and with some computers and MIDI interfaces you would need to use your own routine to monitor the MIDI input, wait for a byte to be detected, and then read it and place it in a variable.

The next line ANDs X with 255 (11111111 in binary), which may seem a bit pointless. In theory, this will not alter the value of X, which is only an eight bit binary number. Due to a peculiarity of the ST MIDI interface and many ST programming languages, the returned value is actually a sixteen bit number which has what always seems to be 11111111 as the eight most significant bits. There is actually no problem if you read a sixteen bit value from the MIDI port, and then write it to the MIDI output. The upper eight bits are simply stripped off the number, and the correct eight bit value will be sent. However, if you are undertaking conditional instructions that rely on the processed values being eight bit types (which we are in this case), the unwanted eight most significant bits must be stripped from the value before it is used in a conditional instruction. This is achieved by ANDing it with 255. It is not unusual for computer software and equipment to operate in a something less than entirely straightforward manner, and you need to be on your guard against this sort of thing.

The rest of this program line checks to see if the received value is not equal to 248 (the decimal value for a MIDI clock message byte), and outputs it to the MIDI port provided it is not equal to this value. In other words, the program passes all bytes except MIDI clock types through to the MIDI output, giving the desired filtering. Again, having a built-in MIDI port that is properly supported by the programming language makes writing data to the MIDI port very straightforward. With some computers and MIDI interfaces you might need to use your own routine to ensure that the flow of data to the interface is handled correctly. On the other hand, in a MIDI processing application that does not generate any additional data, but does remove some, it should not be possible to write data to the port at a faster rate than it can send it. This should simplify matters somewhat.

With MIDI ports that have a buffer in which data is stored until it has been read, you can sometimes find that a lot of "garbage" is read when a program of this type is first run. There may be no apparent source for this spurious data, but it can be produced in a number of ways. One of these is simply someone accidentally leaning on a keyboard, or something of this nature. It is also possible for instruments to produce a byte or two of random data from their MIDI ports when they are first switched on, although most units are designed to avoid this. Probably the main cause is adjustments made to something in the system prior to running the program. With many MIDI instruments and other MIDI equipped units, operating virtually any control, apart from the volume and tone types, is apt to generate MIDI data. Switching from one sound to another for example, will often result in a program change message being sent. If you have to cycle the unit through several sounds in order to reach the one you want, each step in the process may well generate a program change message.

A simple solution to the problem is to include a routine at the beginning of each program to flush the MIDI input buffer of any data it might contain. This will prevent anything unexpected happening when the program is run. This is a suitable flush routine for use ahead of the MIDI clock filter program.

```
FOR X = 1 TO 256
IF INPSTAT(3) THEN DUMP = INP(3)
NEXT
```

This program uses a FOR ... NEXT structure to loop 256 times, reading the MIDI port each time and dumping the read values into a dummy variable called DUMP. There is a slight problem with this basic scheme of things in that if there should be no data to read, the program would simply grind to a halt and wait for some data to be read. This is avoided by using the INPSTAT function to determine if there is any data to be read. There is no attempt to read the data and dump it into the variable if there is no data to be read. The routine therefore reads and dumps any buffered bytes, up to a maximum of 256, but does nothing on any loops performed after the last byte of data has been read. In order to ensure that the buffer will be flushed, the number of loops must be at least equal to the number of bytes in the buffer.

Pitch wheel filter

It was possible to make the MIDI clock filter program very simple indeed because MIDI clock messages are single byte types, having no data bytes to contend with. Most MIDI messages are of the two or three byte variety, which often makes them a little more difficult to deal with. As an example, suppose that it was pitch wheel change messages that had to be filtered. This type of message has a three byte structure. The pitch wheel change header byte is followed by two data bytes which combine to give a 14 bit pitch change amount. It is obviously not satisfactory to simply remove the header bytes and leave the data bytes intact. These headerless messages could cause a malfunction in any device that receives them.

In practice it is unlikely that there would be any problem, and faced with this type of thing, most MIDI units simply ignore the superfluous data bytes, perhaps displaying a "MIDI ERROR" message to warn the user that there is a MIDI fault of some kind. However, it is not good practice to deliberately produce erroneous data. The MIDI standard allows for one header byte to be followed by more than one set of data, and things might just go very wrong with the unfiltered data bytes being interpreted as belonging to note on and note off messages. You should always endeavour to do things correctly, rather than taking short cuts and hoping for the best.

This simple Fast BASIC program for the ST will provide filtering of pitch wheel change messages, including both data bytes.

```
REPEAT
X = INP(3)
Y = (X AND 240)
IF Y = 224 THEN PROCFILTER ELSE OUT 3,X
UNTIL FALSE
DEF PROCFILTER
DUMP = INP(3)
DUMP = INP(3)
ENDPROC
```

Again, a REPEAT... UNTIL loop is used to loop the program indefinitely. Values read from the MIDI port are placed in variable X. Variable Y is obtained by ANDing X with 240, which strips the least significant nibble from each value. The next line tests to see if Y has a value of 224, and it will have this value only if the byte being processed is the header byte of a pitch change message. If it has a value other than 224, the program simply continues the main routine, and outputs the byte in X on the MIDI output. Therefore, except when a pitch change header byte is detected, the program simply takes data in on the MIDI input, and then almost immediately outputs it again on the MIDI output.

The situation is different if a pitch change status byte is detected. The program is then branched to a procedure (PROCFILTER), or what in general programming terminology is just a form of sub-program or subroutine. For simple programs a structured approach to programming is less important than when producing a major item of software. It generally represents the most simple way of handling things though. Also, if the initial program fails to give the desired result, or you should wish to add to or in some way modify the program, this is generally more easily achieved if you start with a program that is logically structured.

There is a drawback to the structured approach for this type of program, which is simply that structured programs often run significantly slower than the non-structured variety. Speed is often an important factor with MIDI programs, where there can be as many as a few thousand bytes per second to process, and the computer will probably be continuously breaking out into interrupt routines. Modern programming languages mostly run highly structured programs at high speed, and particularly with simple routines, using a structured approach is not likely to produce any speed problems. If you use a programming language that is not very modern, and you end up with numerous subroutines, you might find that the program grinds along very much more slowly than you expected. With this very simple example program and its single sub-program there seems to be no obvious problem with a lack of operating speed, even though the program is written in an interpreted language. The programming language is a relatively fast one though, and it runs on a fairly fast computer. Getting sufficient operating speed is not always so easy, and may require simple and direct methods to be adopted.

The procedure in this program simply reads in two bytes from the MIDI port and discards them in the dummy variable called DUMP. These should be the two data bytes for a pitch change message. Since neither these nor the header byte are transmitted from the MIDI port, the required filtering of pitch change messages, data bytes and all, is obtained.

There is actually a slight flaw in this basic arrangement, in that MIDI clock signals and other system real-time messages can be sent in the middle of other MIDI messages. If this type of data is not being sent by the controller, then the program should work perfectly. However, in order to be certain that it would always operate properly, the procedure would need to be expanded to check that bytes read from the MIDI port were data types. It would have to be designed to dump two data bytes, while passing to the MIDI output any that were found to be header bytes. You might like to work out a routine that would handle this.

All change

In the previous examples we have been removing MIDI messages, but it is not difficult to use a computer to generate messages, or to selectively alter messages it passes. To generate messages, the program can consist just of a simple loop that outputs a series of values to the MIDI port. The values, of course, must be chosen to provide the required MIDI message or messages. This could be something as fundamental as three bytes to set a MIDI control at the required setting, or a complex set of parameters sent as a system exclusive message.

Doctoring MIDI messages needs somewhat more careful planning, but with a program a few lines long you can change any MIDI message to any other MIDI message. This Fast BASIC example for the Atari STs changes pitch wheel messages to MIDI control number 7 (master volume) messages.

```
REPEAT
X = INP(3)
Y = (X AND 240)
IF Y = 224 THEN PROCCHANGE ELSE OUT 3,X
UNTIL FALSE
DEF PROCCHANGE
Z = (X AND 15)
OUT 3,(176 + Z)
OUT 3,7
```

```
DUMP = INP(3)
DUMP = INP(3)
OUT 3,DUMP
ENDPROC
```

The main routine is the same as in the previous program, and it simply passes messages through the computer unless a pitch change header byte is detected. In this event it branches to the procedure, "PROCCHANGE". This first strips the most significant nibble from the header byte so that only the channel number is left. A value of 176 plus this channel number is then sent on the MIDI output. This is a MIDI control change header byte on the same channel as the received pitch wheel change message. Next a value of seven is sent on the MIDI output, which is the control number to be altered. Control number 7 is normally the master volume, and is a convenient one for testing purposes, but this could obviously be any control number you like.

Pitch wheel change messages are high resolution types having two data bytes, with the seven least significant bits in the first byte, and the seven most significant bits in the second byte. MIDI controls are paired so that although each one gives only seven bit resolution, a pair of them together can be used to provide high resolution. Obviously the two bytes of data in the pitch wheel message could be sent in a pair of control change messages. This is usually pointless in practice since most MIDI units implement only low resolution.

Consequently, in this case the first data byte (containing the least significant seven bits) is dumped into the variable called DUMP. The second data byte is also placed in DUMP, but it is then sent to the MIDI port. The program therefore takes in a pitch wheel change message, and in its place sends a MIDI control change message on the same channel, with control number seven being given a value taken from the most significant byte of the pitch wheel message. In practice, this usually means that the pitch wheel will control the master volume of any instruments slaved via the ST computer.

Final points
With the aid of a computer having a MIDI interface you can obtain practically any desired form of MIDI processing, and your imagination is

likely to be the only limiting factor. In order to undertake this type of thing though, you must have a good background knowledge of MIDI messages, and the way they are coded. Whereas most programming deals with whole bytes, with this type of processing you will often have to operate on the data on a bit-by-bit basis.

Many instruments now permit sophisticated control via system exclusive messages, and writing programs to control instruments via this route is one that could be very rewarding. Even if the finished programs lack the professional polish of commercial equivalents, they could still prove to be very useful. Some careful studying of the MIDI implementation charts etc. for your instruments will be needed, but it will probably be worth the effort. If the instruction manual for a MIDI device does not include full details of the system exclusive implementation, the manufacturer or UK agent should be able to supply details on request. Remember that it is a condition of system exclusive messages that full details of them should be published and made available to any interested parties.

8

System exclusive

The provision for system exclusive messages is almost certainly one of the main reasons for MIDI's success. The main MIDI specification caters for all the normal types of control and facilities, but it could not be guaranteed to cope with all eventualities. Although it could be argued that system exclusive messages, by virtue of their non-standard nature, go against the spirit of MIDI (which was designed to let any instrument "talk" to any other instrument), they are really an essential part of MIDI. System exclusive messages enable equipment manufacturers to implement any facility they like, in the knowledge that it can be made accessible via MIDI.

Standardisation

This does not introduce any real lack of standardisation. It is certainly true that special features on an instrument from one manufacturer can not be accessed via MIDI by an instrument from another manufacturer. This is not really the fault of MIDI though, and is simply due to the fact that the special features of one instrument are totally alien to the other instrument. Details of system exclusive messages are published by the equipment manufacturers, and made available to anyone who is interested. Furthermore, anyone is free to use the coding so that their products can be used with equipment from other manufacturers via the MIDI/system exclusive route.

So far this free access has mainly been used by so called "third party" suppliers, who produce computer programs that make use of system exclusive messages to gain access to the inner workings of specific MIDI units. However, it presumably permits an instrument from one manufacturer to legally swap information with an instrument from another manufacturer via system exclusive messages.

Although system exclusive messages do not in themselves introduce any real lack of standardisation, they can be used in a way that does. Ideally, any features that could be accessed via MIDI without the need for system exclusive messages would be implemented in this fashion. Unfortunately, some features which would seem controllable via standard MIDI messages, are actually implemented via system exclusive messages on some pieces of equipment. I suppose that ideally there would be at least basic access to all facilities, where possible, via standard MIDI messages. System exclusive messages could still be used to give an alternative, and perhaps more sophisticated route into the control circuits of MIDI devices.

Some pieces of MIDI equipment do not make use of system exclusive messages at all, but these are now very much in the minority. Many modern pieces of MIDI gear have the ability to make extensive use of system exclusive commands. It would not be true to say that you need to use the system exclusive facilities in order to use these units effectively. Apart from one or two units that rely very heavily on system exclusive messages, you can get excellent results just using the ordinary universal MIDI instructions. Life can be very much easier using the system exclusive route though, and virtually every MIDI system must include units that have potentially useful facilities that are only available via this route.

If you are deeply into MIDI, and wish to get the most out of your MIDI system, you really need to look very carefully at the system exclusive capabilities of the units in your system. They may be of little or no use, but there is a strong possibility that they will prove to be invaluable.

Down in the dumps

System exclusive messages make it possible to incorporate all sorts of weird and wonderful facilities that can be accessed via MIDI, but what sorts of system exclusive feature are actually available in practice? Some facilities of this type are of a highly specialised nature, as are some of the units that include them. Others, and it is only these that we will be concerned with here, are of a more general nature, and are to be found in many MIDI units in one form or other. I think I am correct in stating that the first system exclusive feature to be implemented was the patch dump facility on the SCI Prophet 600 synthesiser. I think that I am also correct in claiming that this was the first MIDI equipped musical instrument to go on sale to the general public.

Patch dump facilities via MIDI and system exclusive messages have been included in many instruments, and other devices, over the years. This probably represents the most common form of system exclusive facility. It is something that could be accommodated by countless MIDI control change messages, but most equipment manufacturers seem to have opted for a more streamlined approach via system exclusive messages.

There have been attempts to standardise some types of system exclusive message, and these have been given the somewhat contradictory name "universal system exclusive" messages. They are also known by the equally contradictory name, "system exclusive common" messages. Probably the best known message of this type is the sample dump type, which is now supported by many (but by no means all) sound samplers.

There is an obvious attraction to standardised systems, but they have their drawbacks as well. The sample dump standard has been designed to accommodate instruments using various degrees of digital resolution, memory sizes, etc., and virtually any sampler could be designed to swap samples via this standard. On the other hand, this versatility makes the sample dump standard less than straightforward, and in certain respects it is rather convoluted. It does not accommodate all the sample parameters of some instruments, and often has to be backed up by ordinary system exclusive messages to fill in the missing parameters.

Standardising sample dumps is a relatively easy task, since it is basically just a matter of swapping a long series of digital numbers. Some samplers have greater resolution than others, but there is no great difficulty in simply stripping off any bits that an instrument can not handle. Similarly, if sample data is too low in resolution, it can still be used, but will simply not make full use of the instrument's capabilities. If you load twelve bit samples into a sixteen bit sampler you get twelve bit resolution. Although in principle any sample can be loaded into any sound sampler, there may well be strict limits on the resolution that a particular sampler can actually handle. This is presumably due to limitations in the control software of many samplers. This means that in practice it might not always be possible to swap samples between two instruments that support the sample dump standard.

Swapping data between synthesisers via a standard system of data exchange is far less easy. Synthesisers operate on a variety of principles, and a set of parameters for one instrument may have little or no significance to another one of a different type. A set of FM parameters are of little use to a conventional analogue synthesiser for example. It takes some sophisticated software to convert sound generator data for one instrument to corresponding settings for an instrument having a different type of sound generator. In most cases suitable software is not available, and this sort of thing obviously goes well beyond simple data swapping anyway.

Although there may seem to be no point in standardising data dumping on synthesisers etc., there is some advantage in at least standardising the protocols under which data is exchanged. This is due to the way in which patch dumps are normally used. They can simply be used on the basis of sending a set of parameters from one instrument to another. Setting up the sound generator circuits manually for even just one or two sounds can be a long and slightly tedious task. Setting up dozens of sounds in this way would be a very protracted and boring task. Where possible, simply dumping individual sets of sound data, or complete dumps, can obviously save masses of time and effort.

In practice, you may not often need to do this. Most MIDI systems probably use a variety of instruments in order to give the widest possible range of sounds. In order to dump a set of patch data from one synthesiser to another you must have two instruments of the same type, or two instruments of broadly the same type from the same manufacturer. In most cases where two identical or very similar instruments are included in a system, you would need them loaded with different sounds anyway, so that as many different sounds as possible are available. Dumping patch data from one instrument to another is certainly a useful feature, but one that perhaps tends to be overrated.

Database

In my opinion at any rate, there is a more useful way of using MIDI dump facilities. This is to dump the data to a storage device of some kind. A large library of sounds can be stored ready for almost instant recall whenever a particular set of data is required. The storage device can be a special disk drive unit having a MIDI interface and some built-in "intelligence", or a computer having a disk drive and MIDI interface. The latter is almost certainly the more popular method, which is not really surprising. Many MIDI users already own a suitable computer, which can therefore be used as a MIDI data storage and retrieval system at little or no extra cost.

It is worth pointing out that dumping samples and storing libraries of them in this way is a less practical proposition. Virtually all samplers have a built-in disk drive that provides a quick and inexpensive means of storing samples. Dumping them to a computer and then to its disk drive is a relatively slow business (it can take many minutes to send a large sample over MIDI). Sample dumping is intended more to permit the transfer of samples from one instrument to another, and to permit samplers to be used with a computer running a visual editor program.

On the face of it, there is no difficulty in getting an instrument to dump some data via MIDI and a system exclusive message, and to store this in the memory of the computer. It can then be stored on disk, and at some later date recalled back into the computer's memory, and then fed back to the instrument. As the instrument is receiving system exclusive data that it generated, it should be perfectly able to understand it. In reality matters are not always as straightforward as this. In some cases this simple method will work perfectly well. The data can be handled at the computer end by a special utility program, or a sequencer might be able to handle it properly. Although the data is actually a system exclusive dump, with luck the sequencer will accept it like any other MIDI data, permitting it to be recorded in full, stored on disk, recalled when required, and played back into the instrument that originated it.

Some sequencers are not quite as accommodating in this respect as they might be, and they might filter out system exclusive messages. With the more sophisticated sequencers there is usually the option of recording system exclusive messages or filtering them. Provided the filtering is disabled, the patch dump (or whatever) will be recorded properly in most cases. The ability to record system exclusive messages is included mainly to permit sequences to start with a series of system exclusive messages that set everything up in the system in the appropriate fashion for the piece that is to follow. However, there should be nothing to stop you recording sequences that are actually nothing more than a system exclusive message, or a group of these messages.

You can actually use system exclusive messages mid-sequence, in order to change the sounds of certain instruments for example. In practice this might not be practical, since system exclusive messages sometimes involve the transfer of large amounts of data. The duration of a long system exclusive message can be a few seconds, or even several minutes. Remember that no note on messages, note off messages, etc. can be sent in the middle of a system exclusive message. A long delay while system exclusive messages take place will not matter in the time before the sequence proper gets under way, but could keep the MIDI interface tied up for too long in the middle of a sequence. If the system exclusive messages are suitably short, then there should obviously be no problem using them anywhere in a sequence. Bear in mind though, that it might take a short while for an instrument to actually adjust properly to the new data, and that its sound generator circuits could well become inoperative while it does so.

Handshaking

Even when using a sequencer (or other storage device) that is designed to accept system exclusive data, you can sometimes find that little or nothing is actually recorded. This is due to the use of what is quaintly termed "handshaking". Handshaking can be of the hardware or software variety. With the hardware type there are extra connecting wires between the units in the system, and these control the flow of data. This usually operates in a very simple way, with the handshake line being controlled by the receiving device. The line is taken to logic 1 if it is ready to receive data, or logic 0 if it is not. The transmitting device monitors the handshake line, and only sends data if it is at logic 1. This prevents the receiving device from being sent data at such a high rate that it can not digest it all properly.

MIDI has no provision for hardware handshaking, but achieves much the same effect via the software version. This utilises a dialogue between the sending and receiving equipment via the ordinary MIDI data lines. In other words, the flow of data is controlled by messages from the transmitting unit to the receiving one, and vice versa. The exact form software handshaking takes varies somewhat, but it usually operates on the basis of first having the sending unit indicate that it wishes to send some data. If the receiving unit is ready to receive the data it sends an appropriate message in response. If not, either it does not respond at all, or it sends a message to indicate that it is not ready to receive the data. Once the flow of data is under way, the receiving unit can sent a message telling the transmitting device to temporarily halt the flow of data, should it start to become overloaded. A further message can be used to restart the flow of data, once the receiving unit is ready to process further data.

A message can be used to indicate that the block of data has been finished, and can include a checksum value. The receiving unit can check this value against the one it has calculated on the basis of the received values in the data. If the two figures are the same, it sends a message of acknowledgement, indicating that the data was received properly. If there is a discrepancy, the data has probably become corrupted somewhere along the line, and a message is sent to the sending unit to indicate that the received data is inaccurate. A fresh attempt at sending the data can then be made.

Another, and broadly similar, form of handshaking, deals in packets of data. A packet is simply a certain number of bytes. This system operates on the basis of the receiving unit requesting a packet, followed by the transmitting unit sending it. When this data has been digested, a further packet is requested and sent. This process continues until a full set of data has been received. There are variations on this basic scheme of things, and the transmitting unit might send a message to indicate that it is about to send a packet of data, and wait for a message of acknowledgement from the receiving unit before doing so. This could be repeated for each packet. Note that with all these systems the handshake messages are system exclusive types, and that they often include information, such as the total amount of data to be transferred, the number of the next packet of data, etc.

There is a definite advantage in having the handshaking protocol standardised, even if the data contained in system exclusive messages of this type is not. With every manufacturer designing their own unique brand of software handshaking, it is very difficult to store the system exclusive messages in a sequencer, or even using a program or hardware device specifically designed for this purpose. If a device is instructed to send a dump of data, it sends the initial part of the message, and then waits for the acknowledgement from the receiving device before proceeding further. The system will then just hang-up unless the acknowledgement is sent. With a sequencer or basic MIDI storage device the acknowledgement will not be sent, and so the required data will not be sent either.

The problem can be overcome by having the sequencer or other storage device designed to recognise system exclusive messages that require a response, and programmed to send the appropriate responses. With a variety of handshake protocols in use, for this method to be fully effective the storage device must be able to recognise and respond to a whole range of system exclusive messages. This obviously complicates matters, and a degree of standardisation would ease the problem. As things stand, there is no universal MIDI handshaking method, although there have been some steps taken in this direction. Also, some manufacturers have tried to ease the problem by giving the option of using system exclusive data dumps without any handshaking being used.

As the handshaking often seems to provide no useful function, and just complicates the use of system exclusive messages, this simple and direct approach to the problem possibly represents the best way forward. To exchange large amounts of data successfully without using any form of handshaking it is clearly necessary for the receiving device to be able to process the data at a high rate. However, bear in mind that by current computer standards MIDI is not particularly fast, and dealing with up to about 3000 bytes per second is not a great technical feat. In normal use any MIDI device should be capable of handling a continuous flow of data at the maximum rate for an indefinite period. There is no obvious reason why it should not be able to achieve this when handling large system exclusive messages.

In practice

If you wish to use system exclusive messages, the first task is to study the instruction manuals for the equipment in your MIDI system to determine exactly what system exclusive facilities these units have to offer. There are no real shortcuts here, and some careful reading of the MIDI implementation section of the manual will be needed, together with some detailed studying of the part that tells you how to access the relevant features. With luck, there will be a detailed section on system exclusive messages, the features they can access, and how they can be used. Try to determine whether or not these messages involve handshaking, as this may limit their usefulness.

When first trying out system exclusive messages, it is often easiest if the messages are just sent from one unit to a second unit of the same type. This enables you to ensure that you have sorted out the right combination of key presses, and that things are working as expected. Remember that many MIDI devices will respond only to system exclusive messages if they are set up to do so. It is not usually just a matter of telling the transmitting unit to send the data. In most instances the receiving unit must be set to the system exclusive reception mode before it will recognise these messages, and produce any response that a handshaking protocol may call for.

Of course, this method may not be open to you, and it is then a matter of jumping straight in and trying to dump and restore the data via some form of storage device. When experimenting with system exclusive dumps it is as well to bear in mind that these messages often provide detailed access to the circuits at the heart of MIDI equipment. It is inconceivable that by experimenting with these messages you could actually do any damage to a piece of equipment, but you could end up scrambling some or all the data held in its memory circuits. Unless you are prepared to take the slight risk of losing some data, it might be as well not to experiment with system exclusive messages.

There can be great advantages in using these messages though. If cartridges are used to store sound data etc., the cost can quickly mount up. In fact it could soon exceed the cost of buying a hardware storage device, or a computer plus suitable software. If you already have a suitable computer equipped with a MIDI interface, then the cost of using this method of data storage should be very low indeed. Computer disks mainly cost only about one pound or less, and can store massive amounts of data (mostly about 360k to 1.4M). At this price it is easy to afford back-up copies of data. This is something that would normally be prohibitively expensive when using cartridges for data storage.

Facilities for dealing with system exclusive messages vary considerably from one storage system to another. Until recently, sequencer programs tended to be rather limited in this respect, and not all system exclusive storage and retrieval programs were actually that much better. Most modern programs of both types, and hardware storage and retrieval systems, now seem to offer greater sophistication in dealing with something more than simple messages that require no handshaking whatever.

When trying to store system exclusive data dumps it is best, where applicable, to opt for the most simple way of handling things. A system that has the receiving unit request data from the sending unit is likely to cause problems. First of all the receiving unit must be capable of generating the correct system exclusive message, and thereafter it will probably have to handle the handshaking, generating suitable messages when appropriate. Matters are likely to be more straightforward if a dump can be initiated by simply going through the right sequence of key presses on the synthesiser.

If the system simply hangs up without the data dump being sent, or with it being only partially sent, it is probable that handshaking is required, and that the receiving device is not able to respond properly. It might be worthwhile studying the instruction manual for the sequencer or whatever storage setup you are using, as it might have an option that can handle the method of handshaking required. The more popular the synthesiser (or whatever) you are using, the better your chances of the storage setup being able to cope with the handshaking.

It is always advisable to avoid loops that result in the data sent from a device being fed back to its MIDI input. This is apt to give undesirable effects, such as the apparent number of voices available being less than expected. With system exclusive dump messages, where a unit would be called upon to simultaneously dump data and read in a fresh batch of data, it could get the device very confused indeed! Always make sure any THRU facility, or anything else that could cause this problem, is disabled before trying to record a system exclusive data dump.

A piece of hardware or a computer program designed specifically for storing system exclusive dumps will normally not permit any editing of the recorded data. You can simply record it and replay it again. Many sequencer programs provide little more than this in terms of editing capabilities on this type of message. The message will appear in the event editor simply as a system exclusive type, which can be deleted or time shifted. No details of data it contains are likely to be shown.

Some of the more sophisticated sequencers provide editing of MIDI data on a byte by byte basis, enabling any byte to be changed to any desired value. In theory at any rate, with one of these you can get into a system exclusive message and alter any value. In reality matters are not this simple. System exclusive messages tend to consist of an initial series of bytes containing the manufacturer's identification code, a device identification code, etc., followed by long strings of data values.

Finding the right byte in the header part of the message and altering it might not be too difficult, but might not be particularly worthwhile either.

Altering a byte of data in the main section of the message is perhaps potentially more useful, but finding the right byte in a string of a hundred or more bytes could be difficult. There is probably a greater likelihood of making a mess of the message than effecting the desired improvements correctly. There is no harm in trying provided a back-up copy of the message is kept, but editing system exclusive data is something that is likely to be easy only when using a custom program for the device in question.

Deleting bytes of system exclusive messages is something that is not to be recommended. This would shift some values from their correct position in the message, which in most cases would result in them being assigned to the wrong parameter. Adding bytes to a system exclusive message has the same basic effect. With the wrong number of bytes in a message, it might simply be ignored by the receiving device anyway.

Channels

System exclusive messages are, of course, a form of system message, and as such they do not carry a channel number. On the face of it, this means that a system exclusive message fed to a number of instruments could cause all those instruments to respond to it. Furthermore, all the voices of those instruments could respond to a single message. This could be useful, but in general would be disastrous. Probably in the vast majority of cases you would not require all the instruments loaded with the same data, and all the voices of each instrument loaded with the same data.

In practice this problem is never likely to occur. With many instruments the default is to ignore system exclusive messages. They will be accepted only if the instrument is set up correctly. Also, the setting up procedure often involves specifying which voice or voices are to receive the data. Provided any instruments in the system that will respond to the message are set up correctly, only the appropriate voice of the correct instrument should respond to the message.

There is another method of ensuring that system exclusive messages reach only the parts of the system that they intended for, and this is to use what are in effect MIDI channels. These are normally referred to in the instruction manuals as something like "device numbers", so that they are not confused with real MIDI channel numbers. In essence these are much the same as MIDI channel numbers though, and they are used in much the same way. Although a system exclusive message can not have an ordinary channel number, it can include a form of channel number somewhere after the header byte and the manufacturer's identification code. The initial part of a typical system exclusive message would be something along these lines:

Byte 1	System exclusive header
Byte 2	Manufacturer's identification code
Byte 3	Device identification code
Byte 4	Device number (channel number)
Byte 5	Number of data bytes in message
Byte 6	First data byte
Byte 7	Second data byte
....	
Byte 200	Last data byte
Byte 201	Checksum value
Byte 202	End system exclusive message byte

It is very common for system exclusive messages to contain a device identification code after the manufacturer's code number. This is usually essential, since each manufacturer is likely to produce a large number of different pieces of MIDI equipment over a period of years. Therefore, it is necessary to have some means of ensuring that a device responds only to system exclusive messages that are intended for that particular model. Otherwise, in sending data to one instrument, the memory banks of other devices in the system from the same manufacturer could be scrambled by data they were not designed to digest. Obviously it would be possible to avoid this by manually setting the appropriate devices to ignore all system exclusive messages. This would not be very satisfactory in practice, as it would be all to easy to forget to set units in the system to the right mode.

Having ensured that only units which are of the appropriate model from the correct manufacturer will respond to the message, the device number then ensures that the message is directed to the right voice of the unit. The device number will often correspond to a MIDI channel number. A system exclusive message having a device number of (say) 12, would then be directed to whichever voice of an instrument was operating on MIDI channel 12.

Things do not have to be organised on this basis though. Using a single byte to carry the device number there are effectively some 128 channels available. Using two or more bytes it is possible to have any desired number of channels. The device number could therefore be used to send a set of sound data to the appropriate one of perhaps 128 of sound data memory banks. In this case the device number would be a sort of pseudo program or patch number, rather than a pseudo channel number. Of course, these two systems are not mutually exclusive, and it would be possible to have two device numbers, with the first one specifying a channel or voice, and the second one specifying a program or patch number.

The initial part of a system exclusive message can be quite involved, but most users of system exclusive features do not need to get this deeply involved. It is just a matter of first briefly studying the equipment manuals to discover exactly what facilities are available. Then they must be studied in more detail in order to find out how to direct data to the appropriate channel, memory bank, or whatever. Finally, and with a little luck, the correct combination of button presses is used to actually generate and send the message. Provided the sending and receiving units have proper system exclusive compatibility, using these messages is little more involved than using any other MIDI messages.

If you wish to get more deeply involved with system exclusive messages by writing computer software that can handle them and perhaps manipulate them in some way, then you will need to obtain detailed information on these messages from the equipment manufacturer or their agent. You may be lucky, and the equipment manuals may provide the sort of highly detailed information you will require. However, in many cases the manuals will not have the information you require. This is quite reasonable really, since there would seem to be little point in manufacturers spending money on distributing this information with every instrument when it will probably be of interest to very few users. On the other hand, the equipment producers should be willing and able to supply this information, either free or at low cost.

The system exclusive data sheets I have seen have all been pretty comprehensive, giving details on a byte by byte basis, together with details of any handshake protocols. There are usually examples of the hexadecimal numbers sent in a typical exchange of data, with both the transmitted and received values being given where handshaking results in a two way flow of messages. There may well even be a few simple example programs (probably in some form of assembly language), together with diagrams and explanatory notes. In fact there is usually everything needed to permit system exclusive data to be exchanged between the MIDI unit and a suitable computer. The information provided is quite technical, and is likely to be presented in a manner that assumes the reader has quite an advanced knowledge of both MIDI and computing. However, unless and until you have this sort of understanding of the subject, you have little chance of dealing with system exclusive messages at this level.

When looking at system exclusive manuals for your instruments you may find that some bytes of data are not fully explained. In particular, there are often several bytes in the initial part of the message that have no obvious function. These are usually the bytes that carry some form of device code to ensure that system exclusive messages for the wrong instrument are filtered out.

This system exclusive message is the one that is used to set the pitch wheel depth of the Casio CZ1 synthesiser (all byte values are in hexadecimal).

Byte 1	F0
Byte 2	44
Byte 3	00
Byte 4	00
Byte 5	7N
Byte 6	Data
Byte 7	F7

The first two bytes are clearly the start system exclusive header byte and the Casio identification code. The next two bytes have no apparent function, and are presumably there to provide filtering. Alternatively, one or both of these bytes may simply be reserved for possible use with future developments. Whatever their function, they are an essential part of the message which can not simply be omitted. Byte 5 carries the MIDI channel number in nibble "N", and this is followed by the pitch wheel depth data value in byte 6. In this case the data value is in the range 0 to 63 in hexadecimal, or 0 to 99 if you prefer to work in decimal.

It is not difficult to use a computer to generate short system exclusive messages such as this, but it is clearly essential to take care that out- of-range values are not used in the messages. Invalid values are unlikely to cause a major upset, but it is better to get things right first time. The final byte is the end system exclusive message.

Finally

If you wish to use system exclusive messages, step one is to read the equipment manuals carefully in order to find out what facilities are available. This might be heavy going, but there is no short cut here. The system exclusive implementations on many modern instruments and other MIDI devices are quite comprehensive, and going through the relevant section of the manual might be quite time consuming. Looking on the bright side, as the implementations are now mostly quite comprehensive, there is a good chance that you will find at least one or two facilities that are of use to you.

Do not waste time using system exclusive facilities just for the sake it! If you find something that looks to be genuinely useful, then go ahead and use it. Otherwise, do not bother to proceed any further. There are plenty of MIDI users who get great results from their systems without ever resorting to any system exclusive facilities.

In the even that you decide to go ahead and use system exclusive facilities, read the manuals very carefully in order to find out exactly how these facilities should be used. If you wish to do anything more than simple data swaps between two instruments of the same type, or two similar devices from the same manufacturer, you might run into difficulties. Again, study the equipment manuals in an attempt to discover whether the units concerned have system exclusive compatibility.

If you are in any doubt about the compatibility of the equipment, you can always try out a facility to see if it will work. However, when dealing with system exclusive messages remember that there is a slight risk of scrambling data if things go wrong. In the main, erroneous system exclusive messages will be ignored by any equipment that receives them. There can still be problems with messages that are almost but not quite right, or where the message actually sent is not the one you intended. When first experimenting with system exclusive messages it pays to proceed with caution. If everything can be made to work properly, there are some useful facilities to exploit.

MIDI hardware specification

The MIDI specification does not just lay down rules governing the message types and protocols, but also specifies fairly rigid standards for the hardware side of things. The MIDI hardware is basically a serial interface operating at 31250 baud (plus or minus 1%). It is asynchronous, which means that there is no additional line to provide a clock signal or some similar means of synchronisation. Instead, the synchronisation signals are sent with each byte of data. These are the usual start bit, plus one stop bit (no parity bits are used). There are eight data bits, with the least significant bit being sent first, running through in sequence to the most significant bit. This is just the standard form of serial signal used in RS232C and similar serial interfaces.

Unlike most other serial systems, MIDI relies on the switching on and off of a current, rather than using two voltages to represent the logic levels. The "on" current is 5 milliamps, and this represents logic 0. No maximum permissible "off" current is specified, but in practice this would normally be totally insignificant anyway (about one microamp or less). Obviously the "off" state represents logic 1.

All inputs should have isolation provided by an opto-isolator. This component needs to be a high speed type having rise and fall times of 2 microseconds or less.

MIDI ports have 5 pin (180 degree) sockets, but only pins 4 and 5 are used on MIDI input ports. On MIDI THRU and OUT ports pins 2, 4 and 5 are used, but pins 1 and 3 are still left unutilised. Unused pins must be left totally unconnected internally. The use of XLR connectors is permitted as an alternative to the DIN type, but only if the equipment manufacturer makes available adaptors that enable standard MIDI cables to be used with the equipment. In practice this XLR option seems to be virtually unused. MIDI ports should be clearly marked "MIDI IN", "MIDI OUT", or "MIDI THRU", as appropriate.

A MIDI THRU socket is an optional port, and is not a requirement of the MIDI specification. Where a THRU output is fitted, it should provide a direct copy of the data received on the MIDI input. In other words, the received signal should be coupled straight to the THRU socket via a suitable electronic switching circuit, and should not be one that is regenerated by the microprocessor controller in the equipment. This avoids any significant delays between the MIDI input and the THRU socket. Also, in order to avoid delays and consequent smearing of the signal at THRU output, the opto-isolator should be a very high speed type if a THRU socket is included (but no minimum rise and fall times are specified).

MIDI cables should be no more than 15 metres (50 feet) in length, and should be terminated in 5 way (180 degree) DIN plugs. The cable should be a screened twisted pair. In other words, the two inner conductors should be individually insulated and twisted together, and covered with an overall screen. It has to be pointed out that in practice many MIDI leads are made from ordinary twin screened cable of the non-twisted type, and that this does not seem to cause any problems.

The inner conductors carry the connections from pins 4 and 5 on one plug to pins 4 and 5 respectively on the other plug. The outer screening connects to pin 2 of both plugs. This does not result in the chassis of MIDI devices being connected via the screen, which would bypass the opto-isolation at each input. This is simply due to the fact that pin 2 is left unconnected at MIDI inputs. Having the screen connected to the chassis of the transmitting equipment prevents radio frequency interference being transmitted by a MIDI cable.

MIDI IN circuit

Figure 9.1 shows the circuit for a typical MIDI input stage. R1 provides part of the current limiting that sets the correct 5 milliamp loop current (the rest of the current limiting being provided in the MIDI output circuit). Diode D1 is presumably included to provide reverse polarity protection to the light emitting diode (l.e.d.) on the input side of the opto-isolator. However, even without D1, the l.e.d. would be

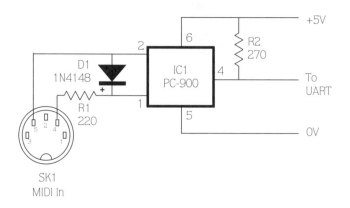

Figure 9.1 The circuit diagram for a typical MIDI input stage.

unlikely to sustain any damage with reverse input voltages of about 10 volts or less. Consequently, this diode is often omitted, and would seem to be something less than essential.

The choice of opto-isolator is important, since the vast majority of opto-isolators are far too slow for this application. Types PC-900 and 6N138 have been found to be suitable. I have also found the 6N139 to be comfortably fast enough, but this device requires a slightly more complex circuit than the one shown in Figure 9.1.

With many opto-isolators the load resistance will be important, and a reasonably symmetrical output signal will be obtained only if this resistor has a well chosen value. The value shown for load resistor R2 in Figure 9.1 is a typical value, but might not suit all opto-isolators.

MIDI THRU circuit

If a THRU output is included it will need a simple circuit of the type outlined in Figure 9.2. This is basically just an inverter driving a common emitter switching transistor which controls the output current. R3 and R4 provide current limiting at the output, and their value is chosen to set the "on" output current at approximately the required figure of 5 milliamps. This splitting of the current limiting resistance into two sections is presumably done as a safety measure, to guard against problems if one resistor goes closed circuit, or a wiring error

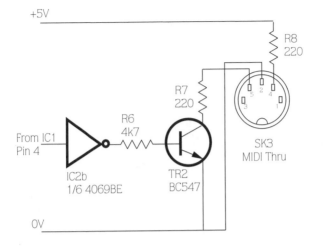

Figure 9.2 Circuit to provide a MIDI THRU output.

results in one becoming bypassed. As there is also a current limiting resistor at each input (giving three resistors in total), there seems to be a slight safety overkill in this respect!

With some opto-isolators it is possible to drive the THRU output (complete with two current limiting resistors) direct from the output of the opto-isolator. Note though, that as mentioned previously, the output load resistance is critical with some opto-isolators. As driving the THRU output direct from the opto-isolator will alter the load impedance when the THRU output is used, this method is obviously inapplicable with many opto-isolators.

MIDI OUT circuit

A MIDI output circuit simply consists of an inverter and an output switch complete with current limiting resistors. A typical circuit is shown in Figure 9.3 (overleaf). The inverter may not be needed, and this depends on the polarity of the output signal from the serial interface device. With the serial interface chips I have used in MIDI applications this inverter has always been required.

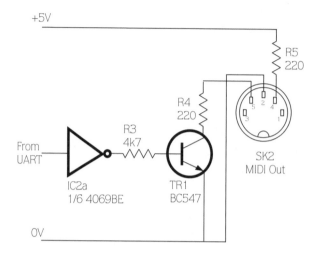

Figure 9.3 A typical MIDI output circuit.

Appendix 1

Multi-outputs and choke

When the MIDI standard was devised, the limitations imposed by sixteen channels and a baud rate of 31250 seemed perfectly acceptable. You have to bear in mind that in those days most synthesisers were monophonic (i.e. you could only play one note at a time). A system having sixteen instruments would probably only occupy sixteen channels and provide sixteen note polyphonic operation overall. In truth, the possibility of things moving on and MIDI choke becoming a problem was foreseen, and the original baud rate of 19200 baud was increased to the current figure of 31250 baud before the system was used in any commercial products.

However, things move on, and in the period of about fourteen years since the MIDI standard was devised the sophistication of electronic instruments has increased enormously. With many instruments now offering eight or even sixteen channel operation, it is very easy to run out of MIDI channels. With many systems now being capable of sixteen channel polyphonic operation, complete with pitch bend, aftertouch, etc. it is also easy to end up with a severe case of MIDI choke.

It has been suggested by a number of people that the two unused pins of MIDI ports could be used to carry a higher baud rate version of MIDI. This would be in addition to the ordinary MIDI interface, so as to provide compatibility with the mass of existing MIDI equipment that would be unusable with the new form of MIDI interface. Another suggestion is that a two speed MIDI system should be introduced. This would have the standard baud rate to ensure compatibility with existing equipment, plus the option of switching to a much higher rate (around 300k baud) for faster data transfers to suitably endowed equipment.

As yet neither of these systems has been adopted into the MIDI standard. Even if they should be, few MIDI users could afford to immediately upgrade to new equipment fitted with one of these "super MIDI" or "turbo MIDI" interfaces. For the foreseeable future, users of large MIDI setups will have to work within the limitations of the current standard.

Multiple outputs

Probably the best solution to these problems at present is, where possible, to use a sequencer that has provision for multiple MIDI outputs. In general it is only the more up-market sequencers that have provision for using multiple MIDI outputs, but presumably anyone having a complex MIDI system would be using it in conjunction with one of the more sophisticated sequencers anyway. It has to be stressed here that by multiple MIDI outputs I do not simply mean a system that has several MIDI outputs, but with each one carrying the same signal. Equipment of this type effectively has a built-in THRU box to enable the star method of connection to be used. Whether the star or chain method of connection is adopted, any problems with MIDI choke will occur just the same.

The type of multiple outputs under discussion here are the type that provide two or more totally independent outputs that can carry totally different signals. Usually this is achieved by having an add-on interface of some kind that connects to one of the computer's ports. I use the C-Lab "Export" interface which connects to the serial port of the Atari ST computers. This gives three extra MIDI outputs, which makes a total of four including the one which is part of the ST computer's standard complement of ports. Note that interfaces of this type (including the "Export" unit) are generally matched to sequencer software from the same company, and are unusable with any other sequencer software. If you wish to use a setup of this type you must therefore seek out a suitable computer – sequencer – interface combination from the start.

Normally each MIDI output is assigned an identifying letter ("A", "B", "C", etc.) so that when using the sequencer you can select the appropriate channel on the required output. With four or five MIDI outputs you have the luxury of 64 or 80 MIDI channels. Unless you are using an extremely large system indeed, this means that each voice of each instrument can have its own MIDI channel. The system is connected up in what appears to be the standard star system, or perhaps with two or three instruments being chained on each output. In effect, each output is a separate system. If there are more instruments than outputs, some careful thought needs to be given to which instruments are connected to which output. Ideally, every voice of every instrument should have its own MIDI channel.

In general, patchbays are used less with a system of this type than they are with other large MIDI systems. If there are a large number of devices in the system, it might be necessary to resort to a patchbay in order to enable a number of instruments to be connected to one of the outputs, and quickly reconfigured as and when necessary. With a large system there is the possibility of connecting the outputs to a patchbay, and then distributing the signal from each output to the appropriate instruments. You must be careful to keep all the output signals separate though, with no accidental merges. Proper merging of the two signals will not cause a malfunction, but it effectively downgrades two 16 channel outputs to one 16 channel type, reducing the number of available channels by 16. It also increases the risk of MIDI choke. Simple mixing of the two signals will cause malfunctions.

I suppose that with multiple outputs, a large patchbay, and a substantial number of MIDI devices, you would have an extremely sophisticated and versatile system. The main problem would be in keeping track of where all the signals were going. There is a lot to be said in favour of having multiple outputs with the number of instruments limited to the point where each voice can have its own channel. This is very convenient in use, with any voice being accessible at any time simply by sending data on the appropriate channel of the correct MIDI output. This gives a standard setup that can handle just about anything, and one that you will soon become accustomed to using. "Usability" is a factor that is often overlooked when setting up computer based systems in general, and electronic music systems in particular. There is little point in having an all singing – all dancing system where you spend 90% of the time trying to get everything set up correctly, and only 10% of the time actually making music!

Choke

Multiple outputs can go a long way to avoiding MIDI choke. If only one output is in use at a time of high MIDI activity, then it would actually be of no help at all. However, this is an unlikely state of affairs, and in practice the activity would normally be spread across several outputs. With the MIDI messages spread reasonably evenly across four outputs, four times the number of messages can be sent before MIDI choke starts to occur. This would normally be sufficient to ensure that MIDI choke will not occur, although it can not be guaranteed to eliminate the problem.

A factor that has to be borne in mind is that MIDI choke might not be caused by the inability of MIDI to send messages at a high enough rate. It could simply be that the microprocessor in the computer or dedicated sequencer is not powerful enough to process the data at a high enough rate, and that this factor is causing the problem. With a single MIDI output this is unlikely to occur, especially with a system that is based on a modern 16 or 32 bit microprocessor. However, with multiple outputs this could conceivably be the limiting factor. Even so, with multiple outputs it would take an extraordinary amount of MIDI activity in order to produce a serious choke problem.

With only a single MIDI output, which is what the vast majority of MIDI systems have, MIDI choke becomes much more likely. If MIDI choke should occur, you will probably be in no doubt about it. At best there will be noticeable errors in the timing of some notes, and tracks might slip well out of synchronisation. In a more severe case there might be notes missing or left switched on. In a very severe case the sequencer program might actually crash, with the computer hanging-up and having to be reset.

If choke should occur, then the only cure is to delete some data so that the flow of messages is reduced to a manageable rate. Some of the more sophisticated sequencers actually have built-in routines that will do this for you. These routines generally operate on a priority basis, with what the programmer regards as the least important messages being omitted, while those that are given a high priority are always transmitted. If a system of this type does a satisfactory job, then you may as well let it get on with things rather than trying to edit the data manually. In practice you might prefer to take control yourself, since the programmer's idea of important data and your ideas on the subject might not be the same. With a sequencer that has no built-in data management system, manual editing is the only option.

Unless you are prepared to accept some simplification of the piece, note on/off messages will presumably have to be left intact. It may be possible to reduce the number of notes without having any affect on the music. Often there will be a track that simply doubles-up on another track, but playing (say) an octave higher or lower. With an instrument that has a transposition facility, or using a suitable MIDI signal processor, it might be possible to play two or more tracks from a single sequencer track. It is unlikely that the amount of data can be reduced by a substantial amount in this way, but every little helps. Often quite a small reduction in the amount of data sent is sufficient to reduce MIDI choke problems to insignificant proportions.

If a clock signal is needed to synchronise a second sequencer (such as the one in a drum machine) to the main sequencer, then it is obviously essential not to switch off the clock signal. On the other hand, if the clock signal is turned on, and there is no equipment in the system that will synchronise to it, then the clock signal can be switched off without there being any ill effects at all. As an alternative to synchronising a drum machine to the main sequencer, the drum machine can be sequenced direct from the main sequencer. This may or may not reduce the data flow. This depends on how many note on/off messages will be sent to the drum machine. It is unlikely to make much difference which system is used. Of course, in order to sequence the drum machine from the main sequencer it must have at least one spare channel, and this factor might force the use of a clock signal and the drum machine's integral sequencer.

The other system messages are ones that will probably have to be left intact. Messages such as stop, start and song position pointers are not likely to be very frequent, and their removal would almost certainly be disastrous. Some of these messages, such as the reset and tune request types, are so little used that they will probably not be there to edit out. One type of system message that can involve large amounts of data which might gum things up are the system exclusive messages. Short system exclusive types can normally be used within sequences without causing any problems, but large messages of this type can take several seconds or longer. These can severely disrupt the timing, probably inserting an unwanted gap of several seconds into the sequence. Normally it is only acceptable to use large system exclusive messages at the beginning of a sequence, prior to the first note.

There is probably little to be gained from removing program change messages. These are normally important to the sound of the music (usually controlling changes from one instrument sound to another), and are so infrequent as to make no significant contribution to MIDI choke.

There are several types of channel message that are normal targets for removal when MIDI choke becomes a problem. Probably the most common target, and possibly the most major cause of MIDI choke, are pitch wheel change messages. These are three byte messages that are produced at a fair rate when the pitch wheel is operated. This can result in large amounts of data being generated in a short space of time. Even so, there should be no problem if the system is handling a few tracks with note on/off information plus pitch wheel changes on one channel. On the other hand, a multi-track sequence with pitch wheel changes on two or more channels is likely to cause problems. So is having pitch wheel changes on one channel together some other facility that generates large amounts of data. Pitch wheel changes are something that must be used sparingly when recording multi-track sequences. One possible solution to the problem is to add some pitch wheel changes manually during playback, rather than including them all as part of the sequence.

Control change messages, of the variable type at any rate, are another possible source of massive data streams. Like pitch wheel changes, when sequencing it might be necessary to put a limit on the amount of control changing that is undertaken, in order to prevent MIDI choke. The importance of control changes to the finished piece is clearly something that will vary from one example to the next, and whether or not to remove any changes has to be a subjective judgement.

With some form of aftertouch now being more common than it once was, it is a feature that is starting to increase the amount of data handled by many sequencers. It should perhaps be pointed out that simply because this facility is present on a keyboard and switched on, it will not necessarily result in any pressure change messages being produced. These messages are normally only produced if a key is held down for more than about a second. Obviously many notes will be too brief for any aftertouch messages to be generated. Once a key has been held down long enough, a rapid series of messages will normally be produced.

The amount of data produced by the use of aftertouch will clearly vary by a substantial amount, depending on the characteristics of the music. Potentially a vast amount of data could be produced, leading to severe MIDI choke. If you make extensive use of aftertouch, particularly the polyphonic variety, and problems with MIDI choke should arise, it is quite probable that the aftertouch messages are the main contributors to the problem. Removing some or all the aftertouch messages will almost certainly detract from the quality of the final piece, but their removal will probably be less noticeable than the elimination of other types of message. Consequently, aftertouch messages are a popular target when removing data in order to avoid MIDI choke.

Something you need to be wary of is removing some pitch change, aftertouch, or variable control change messages from a sequence of these messages. Whether undertaken manually, or by some form of data reducing routine in a sequencer, it might produce rather rough sounding results. Normally the number of messages will be high enough to give very fine control, with no audible steps in volume, pitch, or whatever. If some of the messages are eliminated, this could easily result in audible jumps, rather than smooth changes. It would probably be better to leave the changes out altogether rather than end up with a very cheap and rough sounding effect.

To summarise, the first list that follows shows the messages that should not normally be removed, or which it is not normally worth removing. The second list is messages that can normally be removed in order to avoid MIDI choke, or will have to be removed in order to eliminate the problem. Their removal will probably have some adverse effect on the final piece, but less effect than simply letting the MIDI choke persist. A subjective assessment has to be made as to which messages can be removed without spoiling the integrity of the music.

Messages that should be left untouched

Note on
Note off
Clock (if synchronisation with another sequencer is needed)
Other system messages
Program change
Control change (switch type, mode changes, etc.)

Messages that may have to be removed

Pitch wheel change
Clock and other timing messages (if synchronisation with another
    sequencer is not needed)
Channel aftertouch
Polyphonic aftertouch
Control change (continuous controls)
Large system exclusive messages (other than at the very beginning of
    the sequence)

Appendix 2

MIDI checklist

In general, MIDI lays down a framework for manufacturers to work within, with little in the way of minimum facilities being specified. If a piece of equipment has a proper MIDI interface that conforms to the hardware specification, and it responds to just one type of MIDI message properly, then it can be legitimately described as a piece of MIDI equipment. What this means for the equipment buyer is that he or she should not assume that a piece of equipment has facilities simply because they are part of the MIDI specification. Obviously an instrument will respond to note on and note off messages, but its list of MIDI features might not go much beyond that. In fact it might not fully respond to note on and note off messages – there are still plenty of instruments around that are not touch sensitive and which ignore velocity values.

When buying any MIDI equipment it is essential to carefully study the MIDI implementation chart. This is basically just a list of all the MIDI message types, together with some indication of whether or not each one is recognised by the instrument, and whether or not it can generate each message type. Charts of this kind are usually something along the lines of this abridged example.

Message type	Recognised	Transmitted
Note on	X	X
Note off	X	X
Velocity	X	O
Program change	X (0 to 63)	X (0 to 63)
Pitch wheel	X	X
Poly aftertouch	O	O
Chan. aftertouch	X	O

X = implemented, O = not implemented

The first point to note is that some facilities might be implemented on data received, but may not be implemented when sending data (or vice versa). Sometimes this is what one would expect. With an expander module for example, it would obviously respond to note on/off messages, but with no built-in keyboard it would have no means of generating them. In other cases there is no obvious reason for the semi-implementation of the feature. Aftertouch seems to be a facility that is sometimes implemented only on a one-way basis, as is velocity sensitivity on some older instruments.

Another point to watch is the fine print. There is often additional information that qualifies the basic implemented/not implemented information. In this example program changes are implemented, but only data values from 0 to 63 are recognised or transmitted. This sort of limitation is not uncommon, especially on older instruments, and is simply a result of the unit having less than 128 preset sounds. The fine print will usually include information on which MIDI controls are implemented, and which function is assigned to each control number. It should also include details of any extra MIDI modes that are implemented. System exclusive messages are normally dealt with very briefly. Separate charts normally deal with this aspect in some detail.

Just what facilities are important and which are of little use is something that has no definitive answer. It depends on the application of the equipment, the type of music that will be produced, and to some extent on personal preferences. For sequencing work, I would suggest that the two following groups of facilities are the ones that are of most and least importance (respectively), but obviously not everyone would agree with me. Note that by less important I do not necessarily mean not worthwhile – just of less importance than some other facilities. Of course, the sounds of an instrument are the most important feature, and it would be a mistake to purchase any instrument simply on the basis of its features.

Most useful facilities

Touch sensitivity (i.e. implementation of velocity values in MIDI on/off messages)
Aftertouch (preferably polyphonic)
Wide note range (few instruments provide anything approaching the full MIDI range)
Inclusion of at least modes 3 and 4, preferably together with some form of multi-mode
Implementation of system exclusive messages provided this genuinely provides some useful facilities
Control of at least a few important functions via MIDI controls
Good manuals – easy to set up and learn to use (it is very easy to spend so much time setting up equipment and learning to drive it that there is no time left for music making!)
Implementation of program change messages (also a useful method of control in non-instrument MIDI equipment)
Inclusion of THRU socket
Ability to transmit/receive on any desired channel(s)
Keyboard/velocity split operation
Where appropriate, the ability to respond to all MIDI timing and timing related messages

Less useful facilities

Mode 2
Implementation of system exclusive messages that do not provide at least one genuinely useful facility
Pitch wheel changes via MIDI (usually implemented, but can easily lead to choke problems when used)
Mode changing via MIDI (usually implemented, but probably little used in practice)
Implementation of system reset
Implementation of tune request

Glossary

Active sensing

Not many MIDI devices seem to implement this feature, although it seems to be having a minor revival. The basic idea is for a MIDI active sensing message to be periodically sent by the MIDI controller. If a broken cable or something of this nature results in a breakdown in communications, the controlled equipment will detect the absence of the active sensing messages, and will switch off all notes. Otherwise, any notes that are left switched on will remain so indefinitely.

Baud

This is the speed at which data is transmitted in a serial data system (such as MIDI). MIDI operates at 31250 baud (or 31.25 kilobaud), which means that with a continuous stream of data some 31250 bits of information per second are sent. This is not quite as good as it might at first appear, since ten bits (including timing bits) per byte are required, and typically three bytes per MIDI message are needed. This works out at around one thousand MIDI messages per second. This is adequate for most purposes, but with complex systems it is possible for MIDI to become overloaded.

Binary

A form of numbering system where the only digits used are 0 and 1. This may seem a bit crude, but it is the system used in all digital electronics, and MIDI sends values in the form of binary numbers.

Bit

Bit is an abbreviation for "binary digit", which is the basic unit of information used in a digital system (such as MIDI).

Byte

Digital systems normally operate on 8 bits of data at a time, and a group of eight bits is a byte. Even with a system such as MIDI where data is sent one bit at a time, the bits are still grouped into 8 bit bytes.

Chain connection

See "THRU"

Channel

MIDI can operate on up to sixteen channels that are normally simply called channels 1 to 16. Many MIDI messages carry a channel number, and can be selected by just one instrument (mode 3) or one voice of an instrument (mode 4). Any equipment set with "omni on" will simply ignore channel numbers and respond to all messages.

Channel messages

These are simply the MIDI messages that carry a channel number in the header byte, and which can therefore be directed to one instrument, or one voice of an instrument. These messages include such things as note on, note off, and program change instructions. Messages that do not contain a channel number are referred to as system messages.

Clock

A clock signal (in electronic music) is a regular series of electronic pulses sent from one sequencer to another in order to keep the two units properly synchronised (a system which is mainly associated with drum machines). In a MIDI context the clock signal is a regular series of MIDI clock messages, rather than just a simple series of pulses.

Controller

MIDI controller messages enable individual controls of an instrument or other piece of MIDI equipment to be adjusted. For example, they can be used to vary the parameters of an ADSR envelope shaper (variable controllers), or to permit the low frequency modulation to be switched on and off (switch controllers).

Controller - 2

A MIDI controller is also any device that transmits MIDI codes, and which can therefore control other MIDI equipment. Originally MIDI controllers were keyboards, but these days there are computer based controllers, foot pedals, guitar controllers, and various other types. You do not have to be a keyboard player to exploit the power of MIDI.

Copy protection

This is where a software producer uses some system of data encoding (or whatever) to prevent program disks and tapes from being copied. The idea is to prevent people from copying software bought by their friends rather than buying their own (legitimate) copy. Some disks are copyable, but the copies will not load and run properly. Another method, and one that is popular with the more expensive programs, is to have a "dongle", or "security key". This is an electronic device which connects to one of the computer's ports. Dongled software can be copied, but will not run without the right dongle connected to the computer. The use of copy protection and similar methods by the software publishers is quite understandable. On the other hand, it can be inconvenient to users who are presumably paying any extra costs involved. Many users avoid copy protected software as far as possible, and not due to any dishonest intentions.

Delay

Some sequencers have a delay facility, which enables data for one track to be sent slightly delayed relative to data for another track. The idea of this is to permit instruments to be properly synchronised when one responds more rapidly to data than another. This is not an effect I have encountered, but a delay facility is presumably more than a little useful with a system that does suffer from this problem. Significant delays are sometimes introduced (so it is said) when data passes from an IN socket to a THRU socket, but this is again something that I have never encountered. With a large system using the chain method of connection it is corrupted data rather than significant delays that would seem to be the main danger.

DIN connector

This is the standard type of plug/socket used for MIDI interconnections. Note that it is no good buying just any DIN connector, as there are numerous types. The variety used for MIDI interconnections is the 5 way 180 degree type.

Disk

A computer disk is a device for magnetically storing data (sound samples, songs for a sequencer, etc.), and a disk drive is the hardware that records data onto and reads it back from a disk. Disks enable libraries of data to be built up, and provide a reasonably permanent form of storage (remember that the memories of many instruments and virtually all computers are completely lost when the power is switched off). Cassette recorders are often used as a cheap alternative to disk drives, but are slower and less convenient.

Event

A MIDI event is merely a MIDI message of some kind. Sequencers often have their storage capacity specified as a certain number of events. As "note on" and "note off" commands are separate events, and after-touch or other messages may be involved, the maximum note capacity is likely to be less than half the maximum number of events that can be accommodated.

Expander

A MIDI expander is an instrument that has no keyboard and can only be played via its MIDI IN socket and an external keyboard or other controller. Sounds are sometimes preset and non-adjustable, but some of the more recent units are quite versatile. Originally intended as add-ons for organs, the better expanders potentially have much wider application.

Filter

A MIDI filter is not an audio filter that is controlled by way of MIDI signals. It is a device that connects into the MIDI cable and blocks certain types of message from its output. For example, a filter could be added ahead of an instrument that has only omni modes and will respond to messages on all channels. By removing all channel messages except those on a particular channel, the instrument could effectively be used in mode 3. Many MIDI devices have built-in filtering that can be set to ignore certain types of message (in particular, pitch bend, program change, and MIDI clock messages).

FSK

FSK stands for "frequency shift keying". In a MIDI context this usually refers to a tape synchroniser. The logic levels of a digital signal are coded onto the tape as tones of two different pitches. On playback the tones are converted back into digital signals again. Although all tape synchronisers use this fsk coding/decoding process, this description is normally applied to the more simple synchronisers.

General MIDI (GM)

More correctly known as General MIDI System, Level 1, this is the specification for a MIDI system that can be used to play standard MIDI sequencer files. It goes beyond the normal MIDI specification in that it lays down such things as minimum requirements for the number of notes that can be played simultaneously, and the number of channels implemented. It also gives standard sound assignments for the MIDI program numbers. It is only for those who need a rigidly standardised system so that they can swap music in the form of sequencer files. Others are still free to build up a system that suits their individual requirements, however simple or complex those requirements may happen to be.

Hard disk (fixed disk)

Normal computer disks are often called "floppy" disks, as the disk on which magnetic coating is deposited is far from rigid. A hard disk is a more sophisticated type where the disk is rigid, rotates continuously at high speed, and can not be removed from the drive. The non-interchangeability of the disks is not a major drawback, as the capacity of a hard disk is typically equal to that of about sixty floppy disks. The point of a hard disk is that it gives very rapid access to vast amounts of data. An increasingly popular feature on up-market computers, and also to be found on most sound samplers.

Hardware

Hardware is simply any piece of electronic equipment, including computers and musical instruments. Data or programs used by the equipment is the "software". Data or programs held on ROM are sometimes referred to as "firmware", presumably because they are a combination of software (the data in the ROM) and hardware (the ROM itself)!

Hexadecimal (hex)
Hexadecimal is a system of numbering based on sixteen rather than ten like the ordinary decimal system. The normal numeric digits from 0 to 9 are augmented by the first six letters of the alphabet (A to F) in order to give the sixteen different single digit numbers required by the system. Equipment manuals often give MIDI codes in hexadecimal form, but usually include a conversion table that gives hex to decimal conversions.

Icon
See "WIMP"

Kilobyte (k)
The storage capacity of computer disks and memory circuits is of ten quoted in kilobytes, or just as so many "k". A kilobyte is one thousand bytes of data, or if you wish to be pedantic, 1024 bytes.

Librarian
This is a computer program that stores sets of voice data for synthesisers or other instruments. It enables the required sounds to be quickly selected and loaded from disk and transmitted to the instrument via MIDI.

Megabyte
The capacity of large memory circuits and high capacity disks is often quoted in megabytes. A megabyte is equivalent to 1024k, or 1048576 bytes.

Merge unit
A MIDI device that takes the output from two controllers and merges their signals into a single and coherent stream of messages. Some form of merge unit is the only way in which you can have two controllers simultaneously feeding data into the rest of the system.

MIDI choke
A term used to describe what happens if a system is called upon to transmit more data than MIDI can handle. Exactly what happens when MIDI choke occurs depends on the system, but at the very least it

is likely that the timing of note on/off messages will be severely disrupted. In an extreme case I suppose it is possible that the MIDI controller would crash, and the system would be brought to a halt.

MIDI time code (MTC)
Additional MIDI messages which make it easier for MIDI systems to synchronise properly with SMPTE tape systems. It is basically just an alternative to the normal MIDI timing messages (clock, song position pointer, etc.). It operates on the basis of providing timing information. The times are in hours, minutes, seconds, and frames (up to 30 frames per second).

Mono
In a MIDI context "mono" means that only one note per channel is possible. In MIDI mode 2 an instrument is truly monophonic as operation on only one channel is possible, but in mode 4 (formerly known as mono mode) it is possible for an instrument to operate monophonically on several channels. The instrument is then polyphonic, while it is the MIDI channels that are monophonic. The term "mono" is perhaps a bit misleading in this respect.

Mouse
See "WIMP"

Multi mode
This is an unofficial MIDI mode which enables each voice of an instrument to operate polyphonically on a different channel. It differs from mode 4, which operates with each voice on a different channel, but only monophonically. It is permissible within the MIDI rules since it is effectively several mode 3 instruments ("virtual" instruments) in the same case. Note that the number of notes per channel, the number of channels, etc., varies from one instrument to another.

Nibble
Half a byte (i.e. a group of four bits). MIDI header bytes are effectively two nibbles, with each one carrying a different type of information (e.g. channel number in least significant nibble, message type in the most significant nibble).

Notation program
Also called "score writer" programs, these permit music to be written into the computer in standard music notation form. Some programs of this type are simply intended as a means of producing sheet music, but many now support MIDI, and will operate as step-time sequencers. In fact some will turn MIDI data into notes on the staves, and will operate as real-time sequencers (but will not necessarily work particularly well in this role).

Omni
When "omni" is "on", an instrument will respond to messages on any MIDI channel. When "omni" is "off", the instrument will respond to only one particular channel (modes 2 and 3), or each voice will be assigned to a particular channel (mode 4).

Pointer
In the sense of a song pointer, it is a MIDI message that moves a sequencer to a certain point in the sequence. As a computing term it means an on screen pointer (see "WIMP").

Poly
In a polyphonic mode an instrument can handle several notes at once. In the case of mode 3 it is possible to have polyphonic operation on each MIDI channel. The maximum number of notes available at one time is determined by the instruments – the MIDI specification does not set any upper limit.

Port
A port is merely some form of electrical connector on a computer or other piece of electronics to enable it to be connected to some peripheral device. MIDI IN, OUT, and THRU sockets are all examples of ports. The alternative term "interface" is sometimes used.

Printout
Some programs enable data to be printed via a suitable printer. This is very useful, especially with something like a sequencer program that permits only a small portion of long sequences to be displayed on the screen. Also useful with notation (score writer) programs where it enables conventional sheet music to be produced. However, for graphics output a graphics compatible printer is needed (most programs will work properly with any Epson compatible dot-matrix printer.

Program change
Most instruments and other items of MIDI equipment make use of "programs". In an instrument for example, these are a series of pre-set control settings that give a range of different sounds. Program change messages therefore permit the required sounds to be selected at the appropriate times. Note that other items of MIDI equipment such as mixers and effects units are often controlled via program change messages.

Program dump
Many MIDI equipped instruments have the ability to send out via MIDI the full contents of their program memory, or to provide a program dump. This can be used to send a set of programs from one instrument to another (but they will normally need to be instruments of exactly the same type). This facility can also be used to send data to a computer or MIDI disk drive, and then feed it back again when and as required. There is no special MIDI program dump message, and this facility operates under system exclusive messages.

Qwerty keyboard
A term which seems to confuse a lot of people, it simply refers to a typewriter style keyboard (as used in expanded form on virtually all computers). "Qwerty" is the first six letters on the top row of letters keys.

RAM
This is an acronym for Random Access Memory. If you program an instrument (or a computer) this is the electronic circuit that is used to store the information. The contents of RAM are lost when the power is switched off, but many instruments have a battery to power the RAM after switch-off so that contents of the memory are retained. I have not encountered any computers with the ability to store more than very limited amounts of memory in this battery-backed RAM.

Real-time sequencer
A sequencer where the music is entered into the unit simply by playing it on a MIDI keyboard. The sequencer records the data from the keyboard, which is stored in its memory together with timing information. The ability to change the playback speed is a standard feature.

The more up-market systems permit note values and durations to be edited, and multi-track sequences to be built up.

ROM

ROM stands for Read Only Memory. As this name suggests, once the contents of ROM have been set at the manufacturing stage they can not be altered. The main point about ROM is that it retains its contents when the power is switched off (unlike ordinary RAM). ROM is used for storing data and (or) programs that will be needed frequently. RAM (see above) is what is needed for storing your own data and programs.

Sample dump standard

This is a sort of standardised system exclusive message which enables samples to be dumped from a device from one manufacturer to a device from a different manufacturer. It permits the exchange of information such as loop points, and can handle various word lengths. It is by no means implemented on all samplers though, and in some cases it is implemented in a manner that does not provide truly universal sample swapping.

Serial

MIDI is a form of serial communications system, which simply means that it sends information one "bit" at a time. Parallel systems send data several "bits" at a time, and are usually much faster. They need multi-way connecting cables though, and often have very restricted ranges (a couple of metres in some cases). Although slower, a serial system is more practical for many applications.

SMPTE

This acronym (which is usually pronounced "sumpty", "simpty", or something similar) stands for Society of Motion Picture Technicians and Engineers. In a MIDI context it refers to a type of tape synchroniser. It is one that places regular timing signals (down to small fractions of a second) onto a tape track. During playback these timing signals are converted into MIDI clock signals etc.

Software

Software originally meant computer programs in any form (on disk, tape, written down, or whatever). It seems to be more generalised these days. Sound samples for use in a sound sampler and music stored on floppy disk as standard MIDI sequencer files would now be considered software.

Standard MIDI sequencer files

This is a standard file format that permits MIDI sequences to be transferred between sequencers, even if they run on totally different computers. I have experienced no major difficulties on the few occasions that I have used this system to exchange sequences between different sequencer programs running on the same computer, but apparently others have experienced a few difficulties. Certainly a useful facility for a sequencer to have though.

Star connection

See "THRU box".

Step-time sequencer

This is a sequencer where the music is programmed by specifying the note value and duration in some way other than by playing the music onto a MIDI keyboard and recording the MIDI output data plus timing information. A notation program where the music is placed onto an on-screen stave (or staves) in conventional music notation form is an up-market example of a step-time sequencer. With more simple types the notes are entered in a more simple form, such as "C-2, 1/4 note" for instance. Great if your imagination out-performs your playing skills, but a relatively slow way of doing things.

System exclusive

The system exclusive messages are ones that are designed for use only by equipment from one manufacturer. The header byte includes an identification number so that system exclusive messages from equipment of the wrong manufacturer can be filtered out and ignored. Virtually any feature can be implemented using system exclusive messages, and unlimited data can be included in each one of these!

System messages

These are the MIDI messages that do not carry a channel number in the header byte. They are therefore responded to by every piece of equipment in the system that recognises them. These are mainly the MIDI clock and associated messages.

Tape synchroniser

This is a device which keeps a MIDI system synchronised with a tape recording. This is done by placing some form of timing information on to one track of the tape. This timing information, which may or may not have originated from the MIDI system, is converted into appropriate MIDI clock signals etc. by the synchroniser.

THRU

A THRU socket is to be found on many items of MIDI equipment. It simply provides a replica of what is received on the IN socket. In a multi-unit system the THRU socket on one unit can be coupled through to the IN socket of the next unit (chain connection).

THRU box

Not all MIDI units have THRU sockets, and in particular, they are often absent from keyboard instruments. A THRU box has a MIDI IN socket and several THRU output sockets. In a multi-unit system the OUT socket of the controller connects to the IN socket of the THRU box. The THRU outputs then connect to the IN sockets of each instrument etc. in the system ("star" connection).

Visual editor

A program for use with sound samplers, it draws out waveforms on the screen so that suitable start, end, and loop points can be selected quickly and accurately. Relies on swapping sound sample information via MIDI system exclusive messages.

Voice editor

The minimalist approach to synthesiser controls has made setting up the required sounds a relatively long and difficult process. A voice editor program provides on-screen controls that can quickly and easily be adjusted. New controls settings are almost instantly sent to the instrument via MIDI so that the effect of adjusting controls can be heard, and fine adjustments easily made.

WIMP

WIMP is an acronym for Windows, Icons, Mouse, and Pointer. It is a means of controlling computer programs, where an on screen pointer is moved around the screen using a hand operated controller (the mouse). The mouse and pointer are used to select options via icons, which are on-screen graphical representations (pictures of various instruments so you can select the one you wish to use for example). The windows are areas of the screen which are given over to different functions, or with some computers can even be used for different programs! A WIMP environment makes it easy for inexperienced users to operate complex programs, but only if the software is well designed and the computer is powerful enough to run it properly.

Window

See "WIMP" above.

Word

In a computer sense, this is a group of bits that is longer than a normal 8 bit byte. For example, with a sixteen bit sound sampler, a memory capacity of 500k words means that 500k of full 16 bit words can be accommodated (which is equivalent to 1000k bytes of storage).

XLR

This is a type of electrical connector used for MIDI interconnections on some equipment (generally units that are designed for rough handling on the road). Any supplier of MIDI equipment which uses this type of connector should be able to supply suitable connecting leads as well, together with adaptors to permit standard 5 way DIN MIDI leads to be used.

Index

Other books from PC Publishing

Music Technology Reference Book – Buick and Lennard
160 pp • ISBN 1 870775 34 1 • £12.95
- Collection of essential data
- Convenient single reference source
- Includes hints and tips
- For sound recording, broadcast, live, video, film, and computer industries
- With useful planners and checklists

An indispensable source of information. Assembles in one convenient book the essential facts and figures you will need. Like GM sound assignments, SMPTE and MIDI timecode, sampling and looping, music scales, chords, rhythms, decibel, frequency, EQ charts, electronic formulae and component colour codes. And much much more.

MIDI Survival Guide – Vic Lennard • 96pp • ISBN 1 870775 28 7 • £6.95
- Over 40 cabling diagrams
- How to budget and buy secondhand
- Using switch, thru and merger boxes
- Transfer songs between different sequencers
- Get the best out of General MIDI
- Understand MIDI implementation charts

Whether you're a beginner or a seasoned pro, the MIDI Survival Guide shows you the way. No maths, no MIDI theory - just practical advice on starting up, setting up and ending up with a working MIDI system.

Multimedia on the PC – Ian Sinclair • 192 pp • ISBN 1870775 35 X • £11.95
- Explains what multimedia is
- Free multimedia disk offer for all readers
- Install a CD ROM and a sound card
- Use multimedia in your own applications
- Tells you what hardware and software you need

Introduces the whole topic of multimedia to the PC user. Explains what a CD ROM is and how it works. Create your own multimedia presentation containing text, photos, a soundtrack with your own voice recorded as a commentary, even animation and edited video footage.

Order form

Please supply

Music Tech Ref Book _____ copies at £12.95

MIDI Survival Guide _____ copies at £6.95

Multimedia on the PC _____ copies at £11.95

I enclose a cheque for £ _____ payable to PC Publishing. Add £1.50 for P&P. (£2.50 overseas)

Or please debit my credit card:

Card no _____

Exp date _____

Signed _____

Name _____

Address _____

_____

_____

_____

_____

_____

Date _____

PC Publishing

4 Brook St, Tonbridge TN9 2PJ · Tel 01732 770893 · Fax 01732 770268
e-mail pcp@cix.compulink.co.uk